FOCUS ON

First Certificate

GRAMMAR PRACTICE
FOR THE REVISED EXAM

RICHARD WALTON
Series editor: Sue O'Connell

Pearson Education Limited,
Edinburgh Gate
Harlow
Essex CM20 2JE
England
and Associated Companies throughout the World.

© Richard Walton 1993, 1997

"The right of Richard Walton to be identified as author of this Work has been asserted by him/her in accordance with the Copyright, Designs and Patents Act 1988"

All rights reserved; no part of this publication may be reproduced, stored in a retrieval system, or transmitted in any form or by any means, electronic, mechanical, photocopying, recording, or otherwise without the prior written permission of the Publishers

First published by Nelson ELT 1993 a division of Thomas Nelson and Sons Ltd

This edition published by Addison Wesley Longman Limited 1997

Third impression 1999

ISBN 0 582 29096 1

Set in Palatino

Printed in Spain by Graficas Estella

Illustrations
Ian West

Acknowledgements
My thanks go to Sue O'Connell for her help and enthusiasm during the preparation of this book, and to Roberta Longo for useful suggestions, acting as a sounding board and for looking after Patrick when he was fretful.

CONTENTS

Introduction 4

Unit 1 5
Present simple and present continuous
Relative clauses
Phrasal verbs with **catch** and **live**
Adjectives and prepositions, e.g. furious *about*, delighted *with*, etc.
Wordcheck – objects
Grammar round-up

Unit 2 9
Adjectives and adverbs
The simple past and prepositions of time
Expressions with **do** and **make**
The past continuous
The use of the definite article (the)
Phrasal verbs with **put**
Wordcheck – work
Grammar round-up

Unit 3 15
The present perfect simple
Prepositions after verbs, adjectives
The present perfect continuous
Order of adjectives
Modal verbs: ability
Adjectives with numbers
Wordcheck – feelings
Grammar round-up

Progress Test One 20

Unit 4 21
Steal and **rob**
Modal verbs: obligation
Phrasal verbs with **get** and **break**
Participles as adjectives
Compound adjectives using participles, e.g. *middle-aged*, *long-lasting*, etc.
Wordcheck – crime
Grammar round-up

Unit 5 26
Conditional 1
Prepositional phrases, e.g. *on foot*, *by myself*, etc.
Plural-form nouns, e.g. goods, clothes, etc.
Conditional 2
Phrasal verbs with **wear** and **set**
Modal verbs: permission
Wordcheck – modern times
Grammar round-up

Unit 6 31
Looking at the future – present continuous vs. going to
Will – will be ... ing vs. shall
Phrasal verbs with **let** and **cut**
Wordcheck – technology and gadgets
Grammar round-up

Progress Test Two 35

Unit 7 36
The definite article
The gerund
Phrasal verbs with **bring**
The past perfect
Verbs of perception
Wordcheck – travel
Grammar round-up

Unit 8 40
The infinitive (contrasted with gerund)
Phrasal verbs with **look**
Reporting statements
Phrasal verbs with **get**
Comparatives; the ... the ...
Use and non-use of the definite article
Wordcheck – home life
Grammar round-up

Unit 9 45
Expressing quantity
Verbs + prepositions, e.g. apologise *for*, spend (money) *on*, etc.
Reported questions
Expressing number
Phrasal verbs with **come**
Wordcheck – health, illness and treatment
Grammar round-up

Progress Test Three 50

Unit 10 51
Expressing time
Purpose clauses
Phrasal verbs with **go**
Modal verbs: certainty, probability and possibility
Prepositional phrases
Question tags
Wordcheck – danger, escape and reactions
Grammar round-up

Unit 11 55
The passive voice
Causative **have** and **get**
Prepositional phrases
Gerund and infinitive
Wordcheck – shopping
Grammar round-up

Unit 12 59
Wishes and regrets
Past tense but present idea
Conditional 3
Phrasal verbs with **give** and **take**
Review of tenses
Wordcheck – weddings
Grammar round-up

Progress Test Four 63

Answer Key 65

INTRODUCTION

Focus on First Certificate, Grammar Practice can be used either with the *Focus on First Certificate* coursebook or as a free-standing workbook for learners wishing to prepare for the new Cambridge First Certificate examination. It provides extensive further practice of the main grammar and vocabulary items found in *Focus on First Certificate*. The 12 *units* correspond to the units of the course, and useful cross-references are provided. The book is also suitable for upper-intermediate learners who would like to revise and improve their general English.

The exercises and activities have been designed to be as varied, original and humorous as possible to stimulate interest and motivation. Pictures are used throughout the book both to illustrate language points and to entertain.

Each unit contains several *Study Tips* which highlight the most common grammar problem areas and give useful advice on how to deal with them.

Although this is primarily a grammar practice book, each unit also has a *Wordcheck* section which checks the learner's knowledge of many common vocabulary areas, all of which are presented in the *Focus on First Certificate* coursebook. The Wordcheck activities are as varied as possible, often taking the form of puzzles or crosswords.

The four *Progress Tests*, which come after every three units, provide learners with the chance to review much of the grammar and vocabulary found in the preceding three units. There are score boxes after each exercise and at the end of the complete test, so that learners can keep a written record of their score and assess their own progress.

UNIT 1

1 Present simple and present continuous
(Focus on grammar, pages 7–9)

1.1 Which tense?

Complete the following sentences by putting the verb in brackets in either the present simple or present continuous. Also put any adverbs in the brackets in the correct place in the sentence. The first one has been done for you.

1. That man *is looking* (look) at us in a strange way. Don't worry, he *always looks* (look always) at people like that.
2. Water .... (freeze) at 0°C.
3. Brr! I .... (freeze)! Can't we turn up the central heating a bit?
4. I .... (go) to work by car as a rule but I .... (go) by train this week because my car's at the garage.
5. Why .... you .... (always leave) the top off the toothpaste? It .... (make) me so angry!
6. What time .... your plane .... (take off) tomorrow?
7. .... you .... (speak) Spanish? No, but I .... (learn). My girlfriend .... (teach) me. She's from Madrid.
8. Anna .... (work) in New York for three months. She .... (come) back to Bristol on July 12th.
9. Don't forget to phone me as soon as you .... (arrive) in Berlin.
10. .... you .... (come) to the concert tonight? Yes. Well, don't be late, it .... (start) at 7.30 sharp!
11. He's terrible. He .... (always ask) me for cash and he .... (never pay) me back!
12. What .... you .... (do)? Can't you see? I .... (make) a bookcase for the living room.
13. Oh, that's a good photo! Who's that woman who .... (stand) behind your mother and what on earth .... she .... (wear) on her head?
14. They .... (constantly argue) in front of other people. It's really embarrassing.
15. John! Someone .... (knock) at the door. Can you get it? Sorry, I .... (have) a bath.

1.2 Questions and answers

Match the following questions with the correct answers. The first one has been done for you.

1. What do you do? — G
2. What are you doing?
3. What do you wear?
4. What are you wearing tonight?
5. Why do you speak like that?
6. Why are you speaking like that?
7. Where do you live?
8. Where are you living?

A. I haven't got the faintest idea yet. Is it formal?
B. Well, I grew up in Canada and I've never lost the accent.
C. I'm practising for my new role as an American taxi driver.
D. Just past the church, but you can drop me off here, if you like.
E. With my parents, until the new house is ready.
F. A special uniform with the company's name all over it.
G. I'm a cook in a French restaurant.
H. Just tidying up before your mother arrives, dear.

> **STUDY TIP**
>
> PRESENT SIMPLE TENSE
> • Keep a record of those verbs that are normally used only in the present simple, e.g. know, love, want.

2 Relative clauses (Focus on grammar, page 13)

2.1 Matching up

Complete the following sentences by choosing the second half from the box below. You will need to use **who**, **which**, **that** or **whose** to link the two halves. You will also need to change the second part of the sentence. The first one has been done.

> it causes malaria
> your wife used to be a professional wrestler
> they pay her compliments
> its designer used to work with my brother
> they broke the window
> it sells electrical goods
> he painted the ceiling of the Sistine Chapel
> she discovered radium
> you crashed into her car last week
> ~~he wrote Hamlet~~

1 William Shakespeare was the man *who wrote Hamlet*.
2 There's a good shop in Church Street ....
....
3 Isn't Marie Curie the woman ....
.... ?
4 Look out! There's that woman ....
....
5 Was it Leonardo da Vinci or Michelangelo ....
.... ?
6 She adores people ....
....
7 That's the new sports car ....
....
8 Those are the two boys ....
....
9 Actually, it's the mosquito ....
....
10 Aren't you the chap ....
.... ?

2.2 Two into one

For each of the following, rewrite the two sentences as one, starting with the words in italics. You may have to change some words. Be careful with your use of commas! The first one has been done as an example.

1 *Saint Petersburg* is a remarkably beautiful city. It used to be called Leningrad.
   Saint Petersburg, which used to be called Leningrad, is a remarkably beautiful city.

2 *Liza Minnelli* became famous for her part in the film 'Cabaret'. Her mother is Judy Garland.
   ....
   ....

3 Andy bought an *old van* ten years ago. It has never broken down.
   ....
   ....

4 Hideyuki and Kanako met a lot of people in Australia. *None* of them spoke a word of Japanese.
   ....
   ....

5 *Pelé* was the greatest footballer in the world. His real name is Edson Arantes do Nascimento.
   ....
   ....

6 *Elvis Presley* was known as the King of rock'n'roll. He died in 1977.
   ....
   ....

7 A lot of people take this exam. *Not all of* them pass it!
   ....
   ....

8 They gave us *a strange orange-coloured soup*. It had been made by their grandmother.
   ....
   ....

9 It was in 1928 that *Mickey Mouse* first appeared in a cartoon. His original name was Mortimer.
   ....
   ....

10 *Japanese* is rather difficult for foreigners to learn to write. It uses three different types of script.
   ....
   ....

ア	a	あ
カ	ka	か
サ	sa	さ
タ	ta	た

2.3 Right or wrong?

Look at the following sentences and decide if they are right or wrong. If a sentence is right, put a tick (✓). If a sentence is wrong, put a cross (✗) and correct it. The first one has been done.

1 My mother ˏ who says I was a terrible baby ˏ never wanted more than one child. ....✗......
2 My hair, which started going grey when I was 25, is now white. ....
3 My TV, that I bought second-hand, has been working perfectly for over 12 years. ....
4 Her brother, who lives in Australia, has just got married. ....
5 Peter! Here's someone I think you might know. ....
6 It was then that she saw the man whose son had been so rude to her. ....
7 My brother, who lives in Spain, is a journalist. ....
8 The Vatican, that is in Rome, is the world's smallest independent state. ....
9 Exeter, where we both went to university, seems to have changed a lot over the last ten years. ....
10 Did you know that people, who come from Manchester, are called Mancunians? ....

2.4 Commas?

Put commas in the following sentences if necessary. If the relative pronoun can be omitted, put brackets around it. The first one is shown as an example.

1 This is something (which) everyone should know about.
2 Greta found her engagement ring which had belonged to her husband's great-grandmother under the sofa.
3 The Taj Mahal which was built as a monument to a man's dead wife is one of India's most famous sights.
4 The author who wrote all those murder stories has been found dead.
5 The exhibition which takes place every year is always very successful.
6 Ambra phoned me to tell me that the cake that I had made for her party had made everybody feel sick.
7 We went to the Sydney Opera House which is the city's most famous landmark.
8 The ambulance arrived outside the building where the accident had happened.
9 That's the man who we saw trying to break into the shop.
10 Alcatraz where America's most dangerous criminals used to be kept is now a major tourist attraction.

STUDY TIP
RELATIVE CLAUSES
- Remember you only use commas with non-defining relative clauses (giving extra non-essential information).
- Remember you never use *that* in non-defining relative clauses.

3 Phrasal verbs with CATCH and LIVE
(Study boxes, pages 6 and 15)

These verbs can be used with some of these particles.

catch   live   through   up to   up with   on

Using the verbs **catch** and **live** and the particles in the box, put the correct form of an appropriate phrasal verb in the spaces in the following sentences. The first one is shown as an example.

1 The tortoise eventually *caught up with* the hare.
2 I've never understood how such a big family can .... just one small salary.
3 It was a long time before the idea .... , but, once it did, it became incredibly popular.
4 Children of famous fathers or mothers often find it hard to .... their parents' hopes and expectations.
5 Although I didn't understand the language, I soon .... to what they were trying to say.
6 We were so poor by the end of our holiday that we had to .... sandwiches and tea for the last three days.
7 A stranger took her suitcase by mistake and walked out of the terminal with it. Luckily, she saw him leaving and just .... him before he got into a taxi.

UNIT 1

8 His grandparents .... some very hard times when they first arrived in New York with no money and nowhere to live.

9 And now we're going over to Trevor to .... the latest sports news.

10 The new fashion never really .... with the British public.

4 Adjectives and prepositions (Study box, page 18)

Mixed-up sentences

Column A has the first half of a sentence and column B the second half. However, they are not in the right order and the prepositions are missing. Match up the two halves correctly and add the correct preposition. Read all the sentences before you start matching them up. The first one has been done.

A

1 Most teenage boys are keen — H
2 My neighbour is furious
3 The doctors are pleased
4 Mrs Morse was delighted
5 Barbara is very interested
6 Carl is rather bored
7 The girls soon got fed up
8 Everyone was surprised

B

A .... her lovely new car.
B .... learning more about yoga and meditation.
C .... helping their mother to dig the garden.
D .... the litter outside his house.
E .... her progress after the operation.
F .... their decision to get divorced.
G .... working on his father's farm.
H ......on........ one sport or another, usually football.

5 Wordcheck

5.1 Mix up

Match each description of an object with its correct name. The first one is shown as an example.

1 It's a tool you use for digging in the garden. — F
2 It's a thing for drawing straight lines.
3 It's an instrument to show you where north is.
4 It's a thing to help you find things in the dark.
5 They're things you take when you feel ill.
6 It's a device for making doors secure.
7 It's a tool for putting screws in wood.
8 They're things you put on your suitcases with your name and address on.
9 It's an instrument for measuring the temperature.
10 It's a thing you put your possessions in when you go walking or climbing.

A tablets   F spade
B rucksack   G thermometer
C torch   H ruler
D screwdriver   I compass
E labels   J lock

5.2 Oh yes, it's a ... thingummy

Give the correct name to each of the objects described below. Look at the example in number one.

1 It's a tool you use for putting nails in wood.
hammer

2 It's a device for catching fish with.
....

3 It's a container used for carrying and serving liquids at the table.
....

4 It's an instrument for seeing distant objects.
....

5 It's a thing you write notes in.
....

6 It's a thing a referee uses to stop play.
....

7 It's a container you keep in your house or car to be used if someone has an accident.
....

8 They're for cutting paper or material with.
....

9 It's a thing you use for keeping your neck warm.
....

10 It's a thing for making clothes smooth.
....

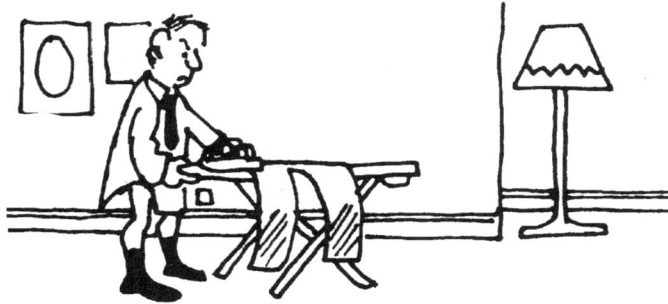

6 Grammar round-up

In the following questions complete the second sentence so it has a similar meaning to the first sentence. Use the word given and other words to complete each sentence. You must use between two and five words. Do not change the word given. The first one has been done for you.

1 Maria likes visiting old churches.
 keen
 Maria *is keen on visiting* old churches.
2 What's your job then, Harry?
 do
 What .... then, Harry?
3 I've got a temporary job in a shoe shop until I go to university.
 temporarily
 I .... in a shoe shop until I go to university.
4 Jeans became popular with young people in the 1950s.
 caught
 Jeans .... with young people in the 1950s.
5 Joe was angry because his sister had broken his cassette player.
 for
 Joe was angry with ....
 .... his cassette player.
6 Venice is slowly sinking into the sea. It is in the north-east of Italy.
 which
 Venice .... in the north-east of Italy, is slowly sinking into the sea.
7 The concert wasn't as good as we had expected.
 live
 The concert didn't .... our expectations.

8 Brad has agreed to play squash with Gerry tomorrow evening.
 is
 Brad .... squash with Gerry tomorrow evening.
9 The party caused great excitement among the schoolchildren.
 were
 The schoolchildren ....
 .... the party.
10 Complaints about the food! That's all I ever hear from you!
 always
 You ....
 .... the food!

UNIT 2

1 Adjectives and adverbs (Focus on grammar, pages 24–25)

1.1 Take your pick

Underline the correct alternative in the following sentences. The first one has been done as an example.

1 Ugh! I can't eat this fish, it smells <u>awful</u>/awfully!
2 She got really angry and slapped me hard/hardly in the face.
3 I'm terrible/terribly sorry but I won't be able to come to your party on Saturday after all.
4 And they all lived happy/happily ever after.
5 That new Volkswagen is definite/definitely too expensive for us.
6 Please stop speaking in such a loud/loudly voice. This is a library, you know!
7 Try some of this cheese. It looks a bit strange/strangely but it tastes really good/well.
8 She still speaks very bad/badly French even though she's been living in Paris for nearly three years.
9 Be careful/carefully! That vase is over one thousand years old, it's absolutely priceless.
10 It is rather unfortunate/unfortunately that they no longer speak to each other, they used to be such good friends.

UNIT 2

1.2 Which is which?

Look at the following sentences and decide if the word in italics is used as an adjective or an adverb. The first one has been done as an example.

1 Why do you want to buy such a *fast* car?
   adjective
2 What a nice man! Yes, he seemed very *friendly*.
   ....
3 When we got home we went *straight* to bed.
   ....
4 Come on you children! Stop being so *silly* and do your homework!
   ....
5 Daniel makes *lovely* home-made bread.
   ....
6 Just before the end of term we all have to work very *hard*.
   ....
7 Kim is the girl with *straight* hair sitting in the corner.
   ....
8 We drove to the hospital as *fast* as possible.
   ....

STUDY TIP

ADVERBS

- Make a special note of those adverbs which do not end in ...ly,
  e.g. hard, well, late.

1.3 Comparatives and superlatives

Complete the following sentences with the comparative or superlative form of a word from the box. In some cases, you will have to create adverbs. Look at the first one, which has been done as an example.

| hard | cheap | intelligent | tiring | thin |
| quiet | happy | ~~quick~~ | attractive | bad |

1 Generally speaking, boys grow up less quickly than girls.
2 Maria is much ...more intelligently........
   .... than her brother. She learns things in half the time it takes him.
3 Look, we haven't got much money so we'll have to stay in ...cheapest............... hotel we can find.
4 Of all the cars we looked at, this is
   ......the most attractively............... designed. It really is very good to look at.

5 They found the long flight on Concorde much
   ...less tiring..................... than they had expected and didn't feel at all tired at the cocktail party.
6 Try and speak ...more quietly............... – your mother's got a bad headache.
7 He still says that the year he spent on Crete away from phone calls, stress and worries was
   ...happiest............... time of his life.
8 At university, he always worked
   ...harder............... than everyone else and got excellent results in his final exams.
9 The weather conditions got ...worse...............
   and the match had to be called off.
10 You'll have to do that again. You know how fussy Grandma is about her food. She likes her ham sliced
   ...more thinly............... than that.

2 The simple past and prepositions of time
(Focus on grammar, pages 28–29)

2.1 Match and add

Match the first half of the sentence in column A with the second half in column B. You will also have to add a suitable link word. The first one has been done as an example.

A

1 I sucked my thumb   [F]
2 Did you try 'sushi'   [ ]
3 How long ....   [ ]
4 Where did you work   [ ]
5 Young people believed in peace and love   [ ]
6 Elisabeth lived in Venice   [ ]
7 He got married for the second time   [ ]
8 We always had a big party   [ ]

B

A .... the 1960s.
B .... twelve years, that's why she speaks such good Italian.
C .... the same day as his first wedding.
D .... you were in Tokyo?
E .... New Year's Eve.

F ....until.... I was nine years old.
G did you give up smoking?
H .... you got your new job at the BBC?

2.2 Life Story

Fill in the gaps in this newspaper article about a famous pop star. Put only **one** word in each gap. The first one has been done for you.

Frederick Bulsara, better known as Freddie Mercury, was born in Zanzibar (1) .....on..... September 5th, 1946. He (2) .... to London with his family (3) .... 1959 and took his first exploratory steps into music with a group called 'Wreckage'. He (4) .... the recently formed band, Queen, in 1970, (5) .... also studying design and running a stall at Kensington Market. The group did not (6) .... a recording contract (7) .... 1972. Mercury always maintained his solo career outside the band. His intermittent solo work over the years (8) .... the Mr Bad Guy album, three songs for a musical and the album 'Barcelona'.
Freddie Mercury (9) .... a great musical talent. In 1975, he (10) .... his first Ivor Novello award for 'Killer Queen' and in the next year the semi-symphonic 'Bohemian Rhapsody' resulted in a second. From then on, everything Queen did was on a monstrous scale. They (11) .... to 150,000 people in London's Hyde Park in 1976.
(12) .... 1982, the band had (13) .... in the Guinness Book of Records as Britain's highest paid executives. In 1990 they (14) .... another award for their contribution to British music.
Freddie Mercury (15) .... in November 1991 after a debilitating illness which lasted over a year.

2.3 You say it like this

The irregular past of each group of verbs is pronounced in the same way. Write in the correct spelling for each irregular past and complete the sentences that go with each group. Look at the example.

A /ed/ bleed .....bled...... , breed .... , feed .... , lead .... , read .... , say .... , spread ....
1 Bill cut his finger quite badly and it *bled* all over his trousers.
2 She .... her cat on chicken and cream.
3 The receptionist .... the way to the manager's office.

B /eɪd/ lay .... , make .... , mislay .... , pay ....
1 Patricia .... the table but forgot the fish knives.
2 I .... my umbrella somewhere and got soaking wet.

C /ɔ:t/ bring .... , buy .... , catch .... , fight .... , think ....
1 We didn't get to the meeting on time because we .... the wrong train.
2 Emmeline Pankhurst .... for women's right to vote.

D /ent/ bend .... , go .... , lend .... , mean .... , send .... , spend ....
1 All her students wanted to know what the word 'bonkers' ....
2 He was so strong that he .... the iron bar with his bare hands.
3 His sister .... him over £15,000 to set up his business.

E /u:/ blow .... , draw .... , fly .... , grow .... , throw ....
1 The tour guide .... a quick map on the back of an old envelope.
2 The bomb .... up seconds after the police had cleared the area.
3 My grandfather .... excellent tomatoes under old plastic bags.

F /ɔ:(r)/ bear .... , see .... , swear .... , tear .... , wear ....
1 Julia was sent home because she .... at the teacher.
2 The thief .... his trousers as he tried to climb over the fence.
3 He .... his pain very bravely.

G /ept/ creep .... , keep .... , leap .... , sleep .... , sweep .... , weep ....
1 They .... with joy when they heard their daughter had been found.
2 The cat .... slowly towards the bird, which was busy eating peanuts.
3 We .... the leaves into a pile and set fire to it.

UNIT 2

3 Expressions with DO and MAKE (Study box, page 30)

3.1 Look it up

Put **do** or **make** in the middle of each of these word circles. Use an English – English dictionary to help you if you are not sure.

A

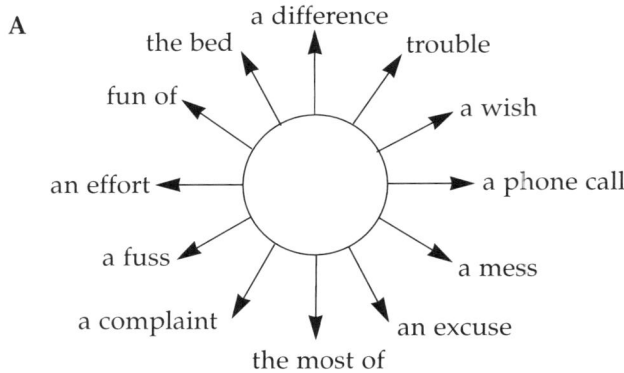

the bed, a difference, trouble, a wish, a phone call, a mess, an excuse, the most of, a complaint, a fuss, an effort, fun of

B

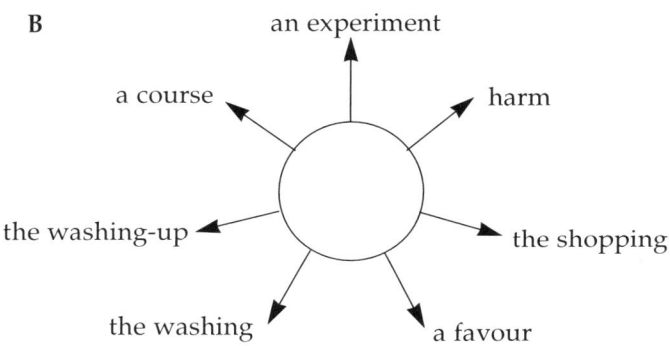

an experiment, harm, the shopping, a favour, the washing, the washing-up, a course

3.2 Do or Make?

Complete the following sentences with expressions from Exercise 3.1. You may need to add an article. The first one has been done as an example.

experiments	~~room~~	trouble	bit	choice	fun
favour	bed	washing-up	complaint	harm
excuse	wish	phone calls	offer

1 If you wish to *make a complaint*, you'd better speak to the manager.
2 The occasional cigarette shouldn't .... you any ....
3 Can you .... Alex? I need £200 by tomorrow.
4 Can you please .... after 8 p.m., when it's cheap rate?
5 Frank is really lazy, he never offers to .... after meals.
6 At school, a lot of children .... Bruce because he had a strange accent.
7 When her old boyfriend arrived at the party, she .... and left as quickly as possible.
8 We .... in computer skills at university.
9 I never seem to have enough time to .... when I get up.
10 Ten of the football fans were arrested for .... in the city centre after the match.
11 Blow out the candles and .... !

STUDY TIP

DO AND MAKE

- Generally speaking, <u>make</u> is used with the meaning of create or produce and <u>do</u> with the meaning of carry out an action, but there are lots of exceptions!
- Learn which words/phrases go with <u>do</u> and <u>make</u> as word partnerships,
  e.g. <u>do</u> the washing-up but <u>make</u> the bed.

4 The past continuous (Focus on grammar, pages 33–35)

4.1 Nick's alibi

It is now 6.30 p.m. and a policeman who is investigating several robberies which have happened during the day is questioning Nick Cash, an ex-criminal, about his movements today. Look at the clock face with the pictures of Nick's actions during the day and complete his alibi. The first sentence has been done as an example.

1 I ......was having breakfast...... at half past eight.
2 I .... at quarter past eleven.
3 I .... at one o'clock.
4 I .... at half past two.
5 I .... at quarter to four.
6 I .... at five o'clock.

4.2 Continuous or simple?

Put the verbs in the following sentences in either the past continuous or the past simple. The first one has been done as an example.

1 Everyone /do/ their weekend shopping when the bus /crash/.
   Everyone was doing their weekend shopping when the bus crashed.

2 What /you do/ when President Kennedy /be assassinated?
   ....
   ....

3 They /get/ lost as they /walk/ through the woods.
   ....
   ....

4 She /walk/ in the park when a dog /attack/ her.
   ....
   ....

5 George /find/ some old coins while he /dig/ the garden.
   ....
   ....

6 The others /have/ breakfast when I /get/ downstairs.
   ....
   ....

7 While we /eat/ dinner in the kitchen, the burglars /steal/ our stereo, records and computer from the living-room.
   ....
   ....

8 When we /arrive/ at the hospital we /rush/ straight to the casualty ward.
   ....
   ....

9 It was a miserable day. Black clouds /gather/ over the hills and a cold wind /blow/ in from the sea.
   ....
   ....

10 Just as I /leave/ the shop, the alarm /go off/.
   ....

5 The use of the definite article (the) (Study box, page 36)

Complete the following sentences by adding the definite article where necessary. The first one has been done for you.

1 We had some very tasty lamb kebabs for ......—...... dinner.
2 Old Tom's never learnt to drive, so he always travels by .... bus.
3 I arrived home on .... last train and you had already gone to bed.
4 Do you remember .... dinner we had in that marvellous little café?
5 The party went on so late that we didn't get home until .... dawn.
6 What time did you have .... breakfast this morning?
7 Trisha does shift work, which means she starts work in .... evening.
8 They had to stop picking plums at .... sunset because they couldn't see what they were doing.
9 Diana always comes to work on .... 8.15 bus.
10 Nocturnal animals are busiest at .... night.

STUDY TIP

THE DEFINITE ARTICLE

- Remember not to use the definite article when talking about something in general, e.g. Apples are good for you.

6 Phrasal verbs with PUT (Study box, page 38)

Put the correct form of an appropriate phrasal verb with **put** in the following sentences. The first one has been done for you.

1 They *put* the meeting *off* because almost everyone had flu.
2 Hurry up! .... your boots .... , we're going for a walk in the mountains.
3 The operator eventually managed to .... me .... to the sales department.
4 They had to use all the money they had .... for their retirement when their son needed an expensive eye operation in Russia.
5 Alice .... seven kilos when she gave up smoking.
6 They sold their house because they couldn't .... the noise from the motorway.
7 The very long hours .... Lucy .... the idea of becoming a doctor.
8 We offered to .... him .... for a week and he stayed for three months!
9 I always forget to .... the tools .... after I've finished with them.
10 This is a non-smoking area, sir. Could you .... your cigar, please?

7 Wordcheck

Working nine to five

The following sentences all contain words to do with jobs. Complete the words. The first one is shown as an example.

1 Jobs which require no *training* are usually called 'unskilled'.
2 The chairman receives an extremely high s............... .
3 Jim quite likes his new job, except for the u............... he has to wear.
4 Sue had a very successful c............... in advertising before retiring.
5 Whenever there's a v............... in the company, at least thirty people apply for the job!
6 While I was an a............... I worked long hours, did as I was told and earned practically nothing.
7 In some jobs you are given an a............... for the clothes you have to wear.
8 The factory remained closed as all the workers had gone on s............... .
9 Once you've paid your rent and the bills you won't have much left from your w............... p............... .
10 In many jobs, stress is the most serious h............... h............... .

8 Grammar round-up

In the following questions complete the second sentence so it has a similar meaning to the first sentence. Use the word given and other words to complete each sentence. You must use between two and five words. Do not change the word given. The first one has been done for you.

1 When I woke up, there was the usual sound of the baby crying.
as
The baby *was crying as usual* when I woke up.

2 His aunt let him stay at her house for a couple of weeks.
put
His aunt .... for a couple of weeks.

3 He's the best swimmer in the school.
than
Nobody in the school .... him.

4 They took advantage of the strike at work and went to the seaside!
most
They .... of the strike at work and went to the seaside!

5 Two detectives investigating the robbery questioned us for over an hour.
enquiries
Two detectives .... the robbery questioned us for over an hour.

6 I fell over and hurt my arm on my way to the tennis match.
while
I fell over and hurt my arm .... to the tennis match.

7 The children's singing in the chorus was really beautiful.
   sang
   The children .... in the chorus.

8 At school, my reading was very slow and my writing was illegible.
   wrote
   I read very .... when I was at school.

9 As the patient was still too weak, the surgeon postponed the operation.
   put
   The surgeon .... the operation as the patient was still too weak.

10 You should find out definitely what time the exam starts.
   make
   You should .... what time the exam starts.

UNIT 3

1 The present perfect simple (Focus on grammar, pages 43–44)

1.1 Present results and news

Complete the following sentences with the appropriate form of a suitable verb. The first one is shown as an example.

1 I can't come skiing this weekend because I've *broken* my ankle.
2 Sophie .... to Greece several times so she knows the best places to visit.
3 Don't you know about Silvia? She .... twins; a boy and a girl.
4 Oh, no! Guess what! I .... the key so we can't open the door.
5 Why don't you phone her up? Because I .... the number.
6 You'll have to take a candle to bed with you – there .... a power cut.
7 Don't offer Margaret a cigarette. She .... since New Year's Day.
8 Take those muddy boots off. I .... the whole morning cleaning the floors!

1.2 Find and order

Section A has the beginnings of eight sentences. Find the second half for each one in section B. Then put the words in the right order with the verbs in the correct form.

A

1 How many cups of coffee   [D]
2 How many of the candidates [ ]
3 How long [ ]
4 How many boxes of oranges [ ]
5 How much of the damage [ ]
6 How many letters [ ]
7 How many times [ ]
8 How much sleep [ ]

B

A you/for/here/live? ....?
B up to now/type/he? ....?
C already/they/repair? ....?
D drink/so far today/she? *has she drunk so far today?*
E from Spain/arrive/just? ....?
F be/before/we/here? ....?
G since Monday/she/have? ....?
H arrive/so far? ....?

UNIT 3

1.3 What's the question?

Look at these answers and write a suitable question for each one using either the present perfect simple or the past simple. The first one is shown as an example.

1 *How many books has she written?*
Five, I think. And she's writing another one which will be published next year.

2 .... ?
Yes, I have actually, when I was on holiday in Tokyo last summer. I didn't really like it, though.

3 .... ?
Last Saturday. She was looking very well and sends her love.

4 .... ?
Since 1975. I was just a tea boy then and now I'm the Managing Director.

5 .... ?
Yes, we did. It was marvellous. We particularly enjoyed our visit to the pyramids and the Cairo nightlife.

6 .... ?
Nine, so far. The last time was in April when I went to Adelaide.

7 .... ?
Well, I thought it was terrible – slow, boring, predictable. But Bill loved it! Mind you, he always thinks Sylvester Stallone is brilliant.

8 .... ?
No, never. But I'd love to go before it gets too touristy.

STUDY TIP
THE PRESENT PERFECT SIMPLE
- Many other languages use the same structure very differently.
- This tense is <u>not</u> used with a definite past time reference,
  e.g. last week, two years ago, etc.

---

2 Prepositions after verbs, adjectives (Study box, page 46)

Use the appropriate form of the words in the box to fill in the blanks in the following sentences. You will also have to add a preposition. Use each word once only. The first one is shown as an example.

| depend   (dis)approve   ~~describe~~   listen   pay |
| concentrate   complain   warn   rely   opposite   remind |

1 In the guidebooks, the area was *described as* beautiful and unspoilt, but when we got there things had changed dramatically!

2 As with any life assurance policy, the price you pay .... your age and state of health.

3 I wouldn't .... Jim, he never does what he says.

4 His parents .... their marriage because they were both so young.

5 English people seem rather unhappy, they're always .... things like the weather, taxes, the government.

6 She's got this amazing new watch with an alarm that .... her .... the important things she has to do during the day.

7 It was their own fault they nearly died because they didn't .... the mountain guide when he .... them .... the danger of avalanches.

8 His opinion of the play was completely .... mine. He hated it, I loved it!

9 He was so absent-minded that he left the shop without .... the apples.

10 Well, as you know ladies and gentlemen, our lecture this evening is about 20th century literature, and we will be .... the works of the so-called 'Angry Young Men'.

3 The present perfect continuous (Focus on grammar, pages 46–47)

3.1 Present evidence

Complete the following sentences by adding the appropriate form of one of the verbs in the box. The first one has been done as an example.

| fight   try   smoke   sunbathe   ~~sit~~   practise   peel   rain |

1 'Look!' said Baby Bear, 'someone has been sitting in my chair!'
2 Of course it .... Look how wet the road is.
3 'Can you smell that, Watson? Someone .... Russian cigarettes in this room.'
4 Look at those marks on the door. Yes, I'd say someone .... to break into the car.
5 Have you seen your face? It's very red!
Yes, I know. I .... in the garden all morning.
6 Michael! What's that blood on your face?
.... you .... again?
7 Claire seems to be upset. Is anything the matter? No, she .... onions in the kitchen for this evening's meal.
8 I must say your game has improved a lot!
Yes, I .... my service and my backhand.

3.2 Continuous or simple?

Put the verb in brackets in the following sentences in either the present perfect continuous or simple. The first sentence is shown as an example.

1 How far have you walked (walk) so far?
2 Bill and Mary .... (be) married for over twenty years.
3 How long .... you and Javier .... (go out with) each other?
4 Frank .... always .... (live) with his mother.
5 Sorry, I don't know where the manager's office is. I .... not (work) here very long.
6 I'm bored. How long .... Professor Stark .... (talk) for now?
7 How many cakes .... you boys .... (eat)?
8 It .... (snow) all day and it doesn't look like stopping. We'll be able to go skiing at the weekend.
9 Phil and Tony are old friends. They .... (work) together for over twelve years.
10 Sam .... (play) football four times so far this week.
11 Anna .... (drive) the same old car since 1978 and she .... (not have) a single accident.
12 She .... (not see) her old friend Gino for ages.
13 Diana couldn't find a house to buy so she .... (rent) a flat for the past month.
14 I'm really tired. I've got my exams at 4 o'clock this afternoon and I .... (go over) my notes all morning.
15 .... you always .... (live) on your own? No, only for the last eight years.

STUDY TIP

THE PRESENT PERFECT CONTINUOUS
Remember that this tense is not used:
- With verbs which are not normally used in the continuous aspect, e.g. know, believe, want, etc.
  I've been knowing Rob for ages. → known
- With quantities:
  I've been writing letters all morning.
  I've written six so far.

4 Order of adjectives (Study box, page 52)

Do-it-yourself definitions

Think of suitable adjectives (in the right order!) to use as a definition for each of the following. The first is shown as an example.

1 a coin = a small round metal object
2 a record = a .... object
3 a can = a .... container
4 a saucer = a .... plate
5 a sheet = a .... cover
6 a pencil = a .... writing instrument

5 Modal verbs: ability (Focus on grammar, pages 52–53)

Complete the following sentences using **can**, **could**, **could have** or some other form of **be able to**. The first is shown as an example.

1 She couldn't drive home because there was so much snow that all the roads were blocked.
2 Although he was injured in the explosion he .... swim to the shore.
3 I hope we .... talk about this some more when we meet next week.
4 Her contact lens fell on to the floor but she .... find it before it got broken.
5 The receptionist should .... give you all the information you need.
6 He dropped his door-key in the dark and .... find it, so he climbed in through the bathroom window.
7 No one .... speak to Mr Boggins since his release from prison last Thursday.
8 When I was seven I .... put my legs round the back of my neck!
9 He tried to phone her yesterday but .... get through.
10 By this time next year I want to .... speak fluent Russian.
11 There was a serious fire in the bakery but the two men .... get out through a small window in the roof.
12 We .... taken the motorway but decided the country route would be more attractive.
13 When she was a child she .... speak Spanish but she's forgotten it all now.
14 They had such a strange accent that we .... understand what they were saying.
15 Oh, come on, let's go to bed. We .... do the washing-up tomorrow!

STUDY TIP

COULD VS. WAS ABLE TO

- Remember <u>could</u> is not used to talk about one specific occasion when someone had the ability to do something and did it. In such cases you must use <u>was able to</u> (or <u>managed to</u>), e.g. Alison <u>could</u> ski almost before she <u>could</u> walk.
Despite thick fog, she <u>was able to</u> ski down the mountain to get help.

6 Adjectives with numbers (Study box, page 53)

Use the phrases in the bubble below to create suitable adjectives to describe each of the objects or situations described in the newspaper articles and advertisements. The first is shown as an example.

> it lasts three years
> ~~it has three wheels~~
> he's 80 years old   it contains four litres
> it took four minutes   it lasts three weeks
> it has five bedrooms   it lasts 30 hours

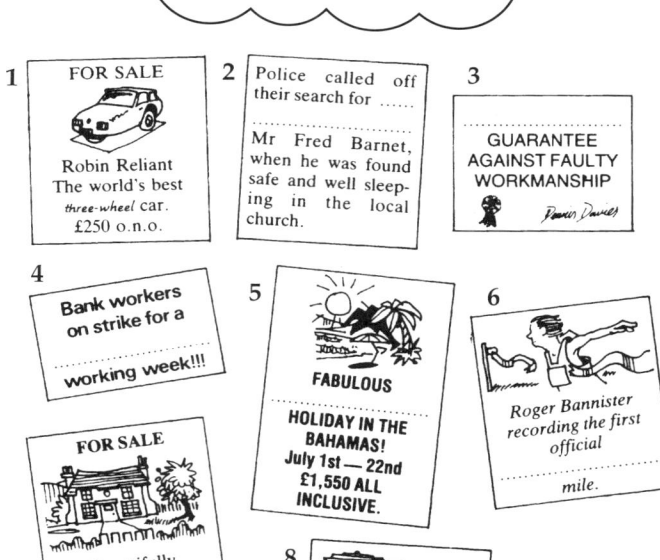

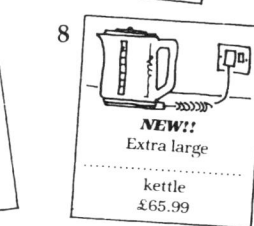

7 Wordcheck

7.1 What a feeling!

Complete the sentences below with a suitable word or phrase from the box. The first one has been done as an example.

aggressive	absorbed	peace of mind
disappointment	tension	~~pride~~	elation
claustrophobia	competitive	exhilarating

1 Helen felt great *pride* when her daughter won first prize.
2 Parachuting was definitely the most .... experience of my life – it was absolutely brilliant.
3 I think you need to have an .... tendency to take up boxing.
4 Joan and Nick were in the lounge totally .... in a game of chess.
5 When I was younger I used to be much more .... , now I just play for fun.
6 Frank refused to go caving with his friends as he suffers from terrible ....
7 There was a terrible feeling of .... after we lost the final by just one point.
8 We all felt a tremendous sense of .... at having reached the top of the mountain.
9 You could feel the .... in the air as we all waited to hear the result.
10 I find painting really relaxing and marvellous for general ....

7.2 Anagrams

Find the names of 12 sports in the anagrams below and then write each sport in the correct column according to the verb you usually use with it. Look at the example in the first one.

1 nurning   *running*
2 migblinc   ....
3 flog   ....
4 nestin   ....
5 joud   ....
6 gastink   ....
7 mimwings   ....
8 drugfinswin ....
9 tosh tup (2) ....
10 burgy   ....
11 sellabba   ....
12 uglynoddibib (2) ....

Go	Play	Do (some)
running	....	....
....	....	....
....	....	....
....	....	....
....	....	....

8 Grammar round-up

In the following questions complete the second sentence so it has a similar meaning to the first sentence. Use the word given and other words to complete each sentence. You must use between two and five words. Do not change the word given. The first one has been done for you.

1 It's a cross-country vehicle with five doors.
door
It's a *five-door* cross-country vehicle.

2 Thomas started working here 12 years ago.
has
Thomas .... 12 years.

3 Their car is French. It's big and red.
a
They've got .... car.

4 I thought she bore a strong resemblance to her grandmother.
reminded
She .... her grandmother.

5 She was offered a job as a teacher but she decided to study law instead.
could
She decided to study law .... a teacher.

6 This will be Daniel's fifth visit to New Zealand.
already
Daniel .... to New Zealand five times.

7 Janet has just come off the squash court, that's why she looks so red!
because
Janet looks red .... squash.

8 We managed to clean up the mess before the visitors arrived.
able
We .... the mess before the visitors arrived.

9 Laura had to pay a fine of 50 dollars because she didn't have a ticket.
   dollar
   Laura had to pay .... because she didn't have a ticket.

10 Rory started working there in 1984 and he's still there!
   since
   Rory .... 1984.

Progress Test One

UNITS 1–3

Check your progress by entering your score in the box at the end of each activity and at the end of the complete test.

1 Read the text below and think of the word which best fits each space. Use only one word in each space.

Beveridge wins National Squash Championship!

Local lad, Max Beveridge, 25, last night (1) .... the Dudley National Squash Championship after a marathon final match with 21- (2) .... old Pakistani ace Imran Younis, (3) .... lasted for over three hours! Max, (4) .... has been favourite to win this championship for several years now, had until last night failed to live up (5) .... his coach's and fans' expectations. But last night was different! Interviewed after the match, Max explained his success like this. 'I've been training really (6) .... as usual with Reg, my coach. I get up at six (7) .... morning, go for a 20- (8) .... run, which takes a couple of hours, have a very light breakfast and then practise my shots and service until about two. I have a few vegetables and a yoghurt for (9) .... and then I do yoga. I think this has helped me a lot. I mean, in last year's final I just couldn't concentrate (10) .... the game, I just kept thinking Reg would be furious (11) .... me if I lost again – and I did! But this time, thanks to the yoga, I (12) .... to concentrate and that made all the difference.'
Max's coach, Reg Clark, said he was absolutely (13) .... with Max's performance this time. 'Oh brilliant, just brilliant! Max (14) .... his best as usual, but this time he had a bit extra up his sleeve.

Watching him today, he (15) .... me of the great Ishwar Chandran when he won the World Championships five years ago – that same concentration and determination. As Max told you, he's been (16) .... yoga for the past six months and this has totally changed his mental approach. This time he wasn't put (17) .... by anything, not even when Imran smashed him in the arm with his (18) .... !'
Reg's final words were, 'Write a good article for the lad, he's had to (19) .... up with enough criticism in the past, especially from me!'
And as one who saw the final, I can only agree with Reg. Max Beveridge seems to be Britain's best hope for the World Championships next August. Let's hope he (20) .... keep his concentration!

[20]

2 Read the text below and look carefully at each line. Some of the lines are correct, and some have a word which should not be there. If a line is correct, put a tick (✓) in the space provided. If a line has a word which should not be there, write the word in the space provided. There are two examples at the beginning.

English is now the unofficial second language of the world. ✓
If you want to do the business in Tokyo, Rio or Dubai the
you won't get far unless you speak some of English. 1 ....
When they go on holiday, people are expect English to 2 ....
be spoken at their destination. But why is English, 3 ....
which until recently it was just a minor language 4 ....
spoken on an island in northern Europe, so important? 5 ....
It can be explained as an accident of the history. 6 ....
At one time people spoke Dutch in New Amsterdam, 7 ....
as New York was originally been called. If that were 8 ....
still true I doubt if English would not be so popular 9 ....
today. So you can see how important accidents are! 10 ....

[10]

3 Choose the word or phrase which best completes each of the following sentences. Put a circle round the letter you choose, as in the example.

Example: I .... I'll pass the exam.
  A wish   **B** want   **C** like   **(D)** hope

1 Mary, ... parents come from Montreal, is bilingual.
   A who's   **B** that's   **C** which   **D** whose

2 Unfortunately, they all did a lot of ....
  A damage   B complaints   C mistakes   D excuses

3 The meeting had to be put .... because everyone was ill.
  A away   B off   C aside   D out

4 They've moved house five times .... 1995.
  A since   B from   C before   D for

5 Although injured, Mandy .... to the village to get help.
  A could walk   B could have walked
  C was possible to walk D managed to walk

6 We bought one of those .... modern coffee pots at the sale.
  A Italian   B stainless steel   C big   D black

7 They .... five candidates so far this morning.
  A 've been interviewing   B 'd interviewed
  C interviewed   D 've interviewed

8 How many times .... to New York last year?
  A has he gone   B did he go
  C had he gone   D has he been

9 Joe seems to be working .... this year than last.
  A harder   B more hardly
  C as hard   D hardest

10 Surprisingly, interest rates .... recently.
   A had been fallen   B had been falling
   C have been falling D were falling

[10]

4 Fill each blank with a suitable form of the word in brackets. See the example provided.

Example: Neil isn't very *interested* (interest) in his job.

1 Cheryl is a really ....(friend) person, she always finds time to talk to people.

2 .... (fortunate), our favourite hotel was fully booked.

3 Mr Donne .... (teach) English literature at the university before becoming a successful writer.

4 It was extremely kind of you and we're both .... (true) grateful.

5 They strongly .... (approve) of smoking and won't allow smokers in the house!

6 I've never .... (fly) before and I'm very nervous.

7 The .... (far) I've ever been from Britain is France.

8 Graeme's a rather strange-looking man with a .... (break) nose.

9 Rachel did much .... (good) in her exams than she expected.

10 It can't have been good news because she .... (tear) the letter up and burst into tears!

[10]

TOTAL [50]

UNIT 4

1 STEAL and ROB (Study box, page 56)

Complete the following sentences with an appropriate form of either **rob** or **steal** and, where necessary, either **from** or **of**. Look at the example given in the first sentence.

1 The two boys broke into the shop and *stole* three radios and a TV.

2 They were both .... while walking through Central Park after dark.

3 His knee injury .... him .... the chance to play professional football.

4 Robin Hood .... things .... the rich and gave them to the poor.

5 Gordon was arrested and charged with .... at the local post office.

6 In the past people were hanged for .... sheep!

7 We think our traveller's cheques were .... our hotel bedroom.

8 The two youths tried to .... old Mrs Kelly .... her pension money, but she defended herself with her umbrella!

UNIT 4

2 Modal verbs: obligation (Focus on grammar, pages 58–60)

Using a suitable verb of obligation in the appropriate form, complete the following sentences. The first one is shown as an example.

1 Poor old Fred *needn't have* watered the flowers; it started raining just as he finished!
2 You .... have a passport to travel from one American state to another.
3 Don't you think you .... visit your grandmother in hospital?
4 You .... ask my permission every time you use the phone – just help yourself!
5 Sorry, I can't come out tonight, I .... go to a meeting at the sports club.
6 We .... asked that man for clearer directions. We're completely lost now!
7 Barbara didn't realise she .... take her shoes off before going into a Japanese home, so she felt quite embarrassed when she was told to take them off.
8 You .... brought your umbrella, it never rains in summer here.
9 She .... called him stupid; he got really upset.
10 That sign means you .... park here. Let's try the next street.
11 Luckily, the man in front offered to carry one of our heavy bags, so we .... pay the excess baggage charge.
12 We booked a room but we .... bothered, the hotel was almost empty.
13 Now, don't forget, if it starts raining, you .... come inside immediately.
14 Jimmy, come here! This is a hospital, you .... run around making so much noise.
15 I'm sorry, sir, but you .... be a member to enter the club.

STUDY TIP

OBLIGATION

Look carefully at the differences between:
- <u>mustn't</u> (obligation) and <u>don't have to</u> (no obligation),
  e.g. You <u>mustn't</u> speak. (You must be silent.)
  You <u>don't have to</u> speak. (You can speak if you want to or you can remain silent.)
- <u>needn't have</u> and <u>didn't need to</u>,
  e.g. I <u>needn't have</u> gone.
  (I went, but it was unnecessary.)
  I <u>didn't need to</u> go.
  (I didn't go; it was not necessary.)

3 Phrasal verbs with GET and BREAK (Study boxes pages 61 and 64)

3.1 *Fill-in*

Fill in the spaces in the following sentences with a suitable phrasal verb with **get** or **break**. The first one has been done for you.

1 The news about her divorce soon *got round* the office.
2 They .... the lack of chairs by sitting on wooden boxes.
3 Some vandals .... the school, sprayed graffiti all over the walls and .... most of the furniture in the staffroom.
4 The crime was never solved, so whoever did it literally .... murder.
5 The two prisoners managed to .... in the back of a laundry van.
6 Nobody knows why they .... their engagement, but they no longer speak to each other.

7 Emma flew to Venice. Unfortunately, her suitcase went to Venezuela and she never .... it ....

8 Put those pills in a place where the kids can't .... them.

9 The doctor used such complicated language that they couldn't understand what he was ....

10 The coach .... on the motorway, so the fans missed the first half of the match.

3.2 Match and add

Match the first half of the sentence in column A with the second half in column B, and add the correct form of a phrasal verb with either **get** or **break**. Look at the first one, which has been done as an example.

A

1 This cold wet weather — D
2 The French attacker .... the defence
3 When Mary lost her job at the hospital
4 The muggers beat up the man
5 His sister .... in tears
6 Bob and Penny, who seemed so much in love, have ....
7 At election time, politicians spend a great deal of money
8 The wardens caught the prisoner

B

A and scored a fantastic goal.
B and .... his wallet, watch and wedding ring.
C trying to .... of his cell.
D really *gets* me *down*!
E trying to .... their message .... to the voters.
F the family found it hard to ....
G when they told her about the accident.
H after going out together for three years; everyone is amazed!

4 Participles as adjectives (Focus on grammar, pages 68-69)

4.1 Hidden words

In the grid below there are 10 present or past participles which can be used as adjectives. They are hidden horizontally, vertically and diagonally. Find the adjectives and put each one in the correct sentence. The first one is shown as an example.

```
T E X C I T I N G O T
O M A W P W O R D W O
F B D F N R B Z K R Q
F A C Q U I R E D I U
O R S U N T O N A T R
B R S C L T K A M I P
P A C M I E E Y T N O
H S K W I N N I N G A
E S T E G L A T R O N
N I V Y D H I T G Y T
O N O T H I N N I S U
U G V R I M O N G N V
W I P H O Z T H I N G
```

1 Some companies refer to the pens they produce as *writing* instruments!

2 Stavros cut his foot quite badly when he trod on some .... glass on the beach.

3 Some people say that Indian cuisine is an .... taste.

4 I read a .... article about how to learn a foreign language in four weeks in the paper this morning.

5 My parachute jump was an .... experience, to say the least!

6 Candidates are invited to send a hand-.................... letter of application with details of previous experience.

7 The coach has included all the same players as last week, as he didn't want to change a .... team.

8 It was a terribly .... situation; he stood up and accidentally spilled a full glass of red wine all over Sara's new dress.

UNIT 4

9 She's a very happy baby – just look at her contented .... face.

10 There's always a lovely smell of freshly .... bread when you walk into our local baker's shop.

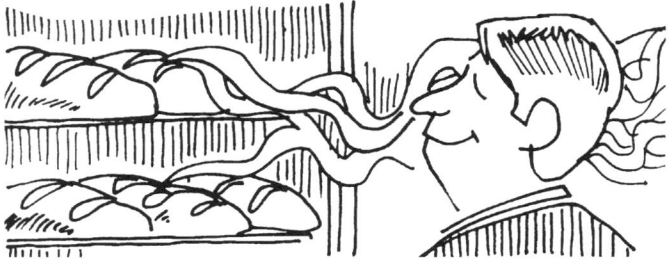

STUDY TIP

PARTICIPLES AND ADJECTIVES

- Remember that adjectives formed with present participles are usually active in meaning and adjectives formed by past participles are usually passive,
  e.g. a boring lesson, a bored housewife.

4.2 Mixed-up sentences

In the bubble below there are eight sentences. Unfortunately, the first half of each sentence has been split up from its second half. Match up the two halves of each sentence and write them in the space provided. The first one has been done for you.

was the boss's nephew!   Having painted the walls, she met an old school friend.
                         was only a copy worth very little.
Having won the race,
                          he decided not to see the film.
I got completely lost in the woods.
                          The person given the job
she was disqualified for pushing.
                          Walking down the High Street,
I could see the body lying on the floor.
                          Looking for a short cut,
The painting stolen from the art gallery
                          Having read the book,
she opened all the windows to let them dry.
                          Looking through the keyhole,

1 Having painted the walls, she opened all the windows to let them dry.

2 ....

3 ....

4 ....

5 ....

6 ....

7 ....

8 ....

5 Compound adjectives (Study box, page 69)

Using one word from bubble A and one from bubble B, create a compound adjective to describe each of the following pictures. The first one is shown as an example.

```
       A                    B
badly      short      sleeved   behaved
hard   long   tight   dressed   handed
 left     badly        fitting   sighted
      short           wearing   sighted
```

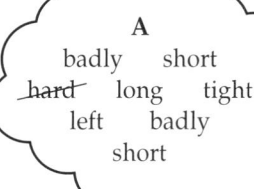

1 a *hard-wearing* boot

2 a .... man

3 a .... person

4 a .... pullover

UNIT 4

5 a .... woman   6 a .... young man

7 a .... shirt   8 a .... little boy

6 Wordcheck

Crime

Look at the clues and fill in the crossword. One across has been done as an example.

Across

1 The police need the public's help to .... crime. (7)
4 On the ....; alert to suspicious behaviour. (7)
6 After two days of questioning, the suspect finally decided to .... to the crime. (7)
9 The police had to .... the man for driving without a licence. (6)
10 across, 7 down: You receive this usually if it is your first crime so, although you are guilty, you don't have to go to prison. (9, 8)
12 A more colloquial way of saying bank robbery. (4-2)
14 If you say someone has committed a crime, you .... him. (6)
16 Hardly any bank robbers use a machine-............... nowadays! (3)

Down

2 If you see a crime, you should .... it to the police. (6)
3 Another way of saying walking slowly, stopping and looking round in a suspicious way. (9)
5 A person who sees a crime being committed. (7)
7 See **10 across**.
8 A person who destroys public or private property for pleasure. (6)
11 Someone who breaks into houses and steals things. (7)
12 An innocent person taken and held by a criminal for protection or money. (7)
13 It means the total sum of money stolen. (4)
15 The place where it is decided if someone is 'guilty' or 'not guilty'. (5)

7 Grammar round-up

In the following questions complete the second sentence so it has a similar meaning to the first sentence. Use the word given and other words to complete each sentence. You must use between two and five words. Do not change the word given. The first one has been done for you.

1 Owing to her poor exam results, she missed the chance to go to university.
   robbed
   Her poor exam results *robbed her of* the chance to go to university.
2 There's no legal requirement to carry an identity card in Great Britain.
   have
   You .... carry an identity card in Great Britain.

25

3 The thieves stole jewellery and paintings worth over £25,000.
   away
   The thieves .... jewellery and paintings worth over £25,000.
4 We saw the film and then bought the book.
   having
   We bought the book .... film.
5 As I didn't know the name for it in Greek, I just pointed.
   say
   Not .... in Greek, I just pointed.
6 The ladies wore evening dresses, but it wasn't necessary.
   need
   The ladies .... evening dresses.
7 The coffee machine stopped working right in the middle of the lunch break.
   down
   The coffee machine .... right in the middle of the lunch break.
8 The wearing of seat-belts is now obligatory for rear-seat passengers.
   have
   Rear-seat passengers now .... seat-belts.
9 Rainy days depress me terribly.
   get
   Rainy days .... terribly.
10 I remember seeing a young man wearing smart clothes.
   well
   I remember seeing a .... young man.

UNIT 5

1 Conditional 1 (Focus on grammar, pages 74–76)

1.1 Did you know …?

Look at pictures 1 to 8 and complete the corresponding sentence using a suitable verb from the box below them. The first one is shown as an example.

| break | hold | ~~get~~ | touch | drop | land | give |
| drop | die | ~~mix~~ | float | stop | get | pour | die | put |

1 If you *mix* blue and red, you *get* purple.
2 You .... a shock if you .... a live electric wire.
3 If you .... a cat, it always .... on its feet.
4 If you .... (not) fuel in a car, it .... !
5 Oil .... if you .... it on water.
6 If you .... a fish out of water for long enough, it ....
7 Plants .... if you .... (not) them enough water.
8 If you .... an egg on to the floor, it ....

1.2 Sort it out

The sentences below have been printed with the words in the wrong order. Re-order the words to make correct sentences. Look at the example given.

1 something suspicious, call you If the police see
   If you see something suspicious, call the police.

2 foggy if carefully Drive it's
   ....

3 a if aspirin you've got Take an headache
   ....

4 first day for at your don't it's too long sunbathe If the beach,
   ....

5 me a you if Give ring a hand need
   ....

6 the cries, him don't If baby up pick
   ....

7 doctor if the Call the pain worse gets
   ....

8 film, what about seen If you've the us it's tell
   ....

9 washing-up Go the you've to done if bed
   ....

10 closer blackboard can't if the Move see you to
   ....

1.3 Link words

Use an appropriate linking word from the box below to complete the following sentences. The first one is shown as an example.

unless provided (that) as long as suppose

1 *Provided* it doesn't rain tomorrow, we'll go for a picnic in the hills.

2 .... Ronald passes his exams, he won't be able to go to university.

3 .... they only accept cash, what will we do then?

4 We'll be home in time for dinner .... the train is late again.

5 I'll take you to the concert on Saturday .... the tickets don't cost too much.

6 .... they don't speak any English, how will we communicate?

7 Your father will lend you the car .... you promise to be home before midnight.

8 .... we repair the roof soon, we'll have serious problems this winter.

2 Prepositional phrases (Study box, page 80)

Put a suitable prepositional phrase in the following sentences. The first one has been done for you.

1 They had to abandon their car in the deep snow and finish their journey *on foot*.

2 Mrs MacGregor has no children so she has lived .... since her husband died last year.

3 If you have small children, you should keep kitchen knives well ....

4 Last century the only way of travelling from Europe to Australia was ....

5 Come on, kids. It's a nice sunny day, go and play ....

6 The bus went .... on the mountain road and crashed into some trees.

7 Politicians always promise that the end of an economic recession is .... , whether it is or not!

8 The old saying '.................... .... , out of mind' means if you can't see something or someone, you don't worry about them.

9 Just as the finishing line was .... , she tripped and fell over.

10 Will you please keep your dog .... !

UNIT 5

3 Plural-form nouns (Study box, page 81)

What's the problem?

Look at the following pictures and using an adjective, write a sentence describing what the problem is in each case. The first one is shown as an example. Look at the boxed adjectives if you are stuck.

1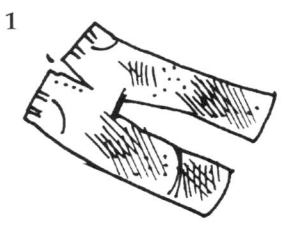
My jeans *are dirty.*

2
The ....
....

3
The ....
....

4
His ....
....

5
Kevin's ....
....

6 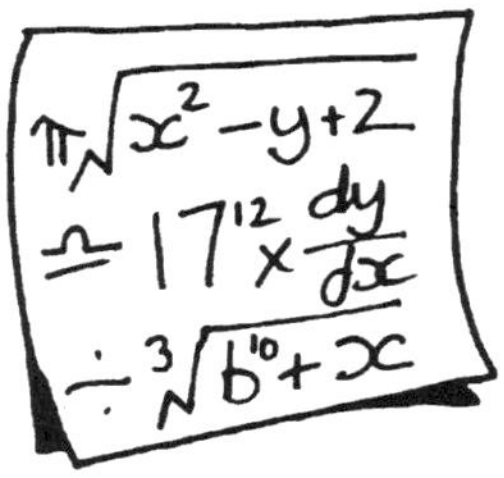
This ....
....

7
The ....
....

8 
The ....
....

9
The centre is old but the ....

10
Michael's ....
....

difficult	broken	ripped
blocked	gone bad	~~dirty~~
shrunk	modern	depressing
big		

STUDY TIP

PLURAL NOUN FORMS

- Make a special point of learning the ones which are used differently in your language.
- Note them down with a short example to help you remember how to use them.

4 Conditional 2 (Focus on grammar, page 81)

Good advice

Read through the following problems and write some good advice for each person. The first one has been completed for you.

1 Matthew and Marion can't go skiing in England because there aren't any mountains high enough.
Well, if they *went to Austria they could go skiing.*

2 My brother gets bad headaches when he reads.
Well, if he ....
....

3 Carol is getting quite fat because she just sits around doing nothing.
Well, if she ....
....

4 Oh dear, I think I'm going to fail my exams.
Well, if you ....
....

5 I find it very difficult to get up on Monday morning after a night at the disco.
Well, if you ....
....

6   Jenny's got a terrible cough because she smokes 20 cigarettes a day.
    Well, if she ....
    ....

7   George and Barbara can't travel abroad because they haven't got passports.
    Well, if they ....
    ....

8   Wolfgang works thirteen hours a day and keeps getting pains in his chest.
    Well, if he ....
    ....

5 Phrasal verbs with WEAR and SET (Study boxes, pages 80 and 85)

Complete the following sentences with a suitable form of a phrasal verb with either **wear** or **set**. The first one has been done as an example.

1   We'll have to *set off* very early in the morning as it's at least a three-hour journey.
2   Giorgio has .... an export/import agency in Milan.
3   My toothache gradually .... as the painkillers started taking effect.
4   Eva was asked to .... her complaint against her noisy neighbours in a formal letter.
5   You should go to the dentist before the decay in that tooth really ....
6   Fergus .... to climb the mountain one Saturday morning and was never seen again!
7   The manufacturers claim that compact discs never ....
8   The police said the workers were very lucky they didn't .... the old unexploded bomb they found in the woods.

STUDY TIP

PHRASAL VERBS

- With certain phrasal verbs, you must put the object pronoun (it, me, her, etc.) between the verb and the particle,
  e.g. make <u>it</u> up, ring <u>him</u> up, etc.
- Make a special note of these verbs as you learn them.

6 Modal verbs: permission (Focus on grammar, pages 86–87)

6.1 Sounds strange or sounds OK?

Decide if the following sentences seem appropriate or not in the context. If a sentence sounds strange, write something more appropriate. Look at the first one.

1   Could I use your phone, Mrs Blake?
    OK
2   I wonder if I might have a glass of water, Mum.
    ....
3   Can I have the salt, please?
    ....
4   Well, can I borrow £250,000, Mr Scott? (Mr Scott is a bank manager.)
    ....
5   Might I possibly borrow your pen for a moment, Pete?
    ....
6   I wonder if I might ask you for some form of identification, madam.
    ....

6.2 What's the question?

Look at the following answers and think of a suitable question for each one. The first one is shown as an example.

1   *Could I have a look at your newspaper?*
    No, I'm afraid not. I'm still reading it.
2   ....
    ....?
    Well I'd rather you didn't, actually. It's very cold today.
3   ....
    ....?
    Yes, you may. But be very careful with it, it's over 200 years old.

UNIT 5

4 ....
....?
Yes, sure. They're in the fridge. Can you bring me one, too? I'm dead thirsty.

5 ....
....?
No, I'm afraid not. I'm expecting an important call at any moment.

6 ....
....?
Yes, of course. Help yourself. There are plenty in the fruit bowl.

7 Wordcheck

7.1 Modern times

Match each word in column A with one in column B to form a useful word partnership. The first one has been done for you.

	A			B
1	traffic	E	A	waste
2	natural		B	paper
3	extinct		C	bottle
4	recycled		D	resources
5	exhaust		E	congestion
6	returnable		F	station
7	radioactive		G	costs
8	bottle		H	power
9	power		I	species
10	fuel		J	paper
11	nuclear		K	fumes
12	waste		L	bank

7.2 What a waste!

Complete the following sentences by putting one word in each space. Look at the example in number one.

1 I can't help thinking that half of the rubbish in my *bin bag* is unnecessary.
2 Plastic is very difficult to d...................... of and can last for hundreds of years.
3 Nowadays even simple things like biscuits can come in as many as three l...................... of wrapping.
4 Half the letters the postman delivers are j...................... m...................... , which I hardly even look at before throwing away.
5 One of the biggest problems is all the sophisticated but useless p...................... that is used to wrap up gifts.
6 C...................... foods such as pizzas or burgers always come in brightly coloured boxes and cartons, which have to be thrown away once empty.
7 Razors, pens, shopping bags, even contact lenses, which used to last for some time, are nowadays sold as 'd......................'. You simply throw them away after use.
8 There is little doubt that in our modern t...................... -a .... society people hardly ever keep things for re-use.

8 Grammar round-up

In the following questions complete the second sentence so it has a similar meaning to the first sentence. Use the word given and other words to complete each sentence. You must use between two and five words. Do not change the word given. The first one has been done for you.

1 She hasn't got enough money so she can't buy that house she likes.
more
If she *had more money, she'd/she would* buy that house she likes.

2 Would it be possible for me to borrow the company van this weekend?
could
I ....
borrow the company van this weekend.

3 If you don't touch those wires, you won't get an electric shock.
that
You won't get an electric shock ....
.... touch those wires.

4 The company was established by our great-grandfather in 1888.
set
Our great-grandfather ....
.... in 1888.

5 My advice is to buy yourself a new car.
would
If I ....
a new car.

6 I've earned less this year than last year.
earnings
My ....
less than last year.

7   At weekends camping is permitted on the beach.
    you
    At weekends .... on the beach.
8   The Wall Street Crash caused a chain reaction in stock markets around the world.
    off
    The Wall Street Crash .... a chain reaction in stock markets around the world.
9   Vicki liked physics best at school.
    favourite
    Physics .... at school.
10 I hope it'll be sunny tomorrow, then we can go to the seaside.
    if
    We can go to the seaside .... tomorrow.

9   How many guests .... (arrive) this weekend? I can't remember if it's 18 or 28.
10 Nancy, can you remind me that I .... (met) Mr Watanabe at the airport at 4.30 this afternoon?
11 Some people say she's just getting fat, but I'd say she .... (have) a baby.
12 It's no good, you can't stop me. I .... (jump)!

UNIT 6

1 Looking at the future (Focus on grammar, pages 92–93)

What's it going to be, then?

Complete the following sentences with a suitable form of the present continuous, the 'going to' future or the present simple of the verb suggested. Look at the first one which has been done as an example.

1   Sorry, I can't come to the party on Saturday, I'm having (have) dinner at Monica's.
2   What time .... the Vivaldi concert .... (start) tonight?
3   Daniela's studying medicine – she .... (be) a doctor.
4   Look out! We .... (crash)!
5   Look at that red sky! You know what that means, it .... (be) a nice day tomorrow.
6   The plane .... (take off) at 3 p.m., so we need to get there by 1p.m. at the latest!
7   What time .... you and Owen .... (play) tennis this afternoon?
8   What .... you .... (do) next Saturday?
    Oh, nothing special. Why do you ask?

STUDY TIP

FUTURES

- Different verb forms are used to talk about the future in English, not just <u>will</u>.
- So it is very important to decide if something is an arrangement; fixed by a timetable; an intention; a prediction, etc.

2 Will power! (Focus on grammar, page 95)

Will he or won't he?

Use an appropriate form of **will** or **shall** to complete the following sentences. The first one is shown as an example.

1   Shall I open the door for you?
2   I'm afraid Mr Escobar is out at the moment.
    Oh well, never mind. I .... phone back later.
3   .... we go to the lake today? It would be a shame to stay at home on such a lovely day.
4   Oh darling, you know I .... love you forever, I .... ever leave you.
5   What time .... we meet?
    How about seven o'clock at the bus station?
6   Don't you touch my car again or I .... call the police!
7   Don't worry, I .... tell anyone about your secret.

UNIT 6

8 Ooh, this bag weighs a ton!
   I .... carry it for you if you want.

STUDY TIP

WILL AND SHALL

- <u>will</u> or <u>'ll</u> is mostly used as a modal verb to make offers, agree/refuse to do things, to make promises/threats, to come to a sudden decision, etc.
- <u>shall</u> is usually used only with <u>I</u> and <u>we</u> in the interrogative when asking for consent or agreement, or for a suggestion.

3 Ways of looking at the future (Focus on grammar, pages 97–99)

3.1 What do you think?

Look at the ideas below. Numbers 1 to 8 refer to you and your life. Numbers 9 to 12 are more general. Think about these ideas 10 years from now, and what changes there might be and write what you think. Try to use most of the words and phrases in the box below. A suggested answer is given for number one.

I'm sure ...	I think ...	I don't think ...	I expect ...
I imagine ...	I hope ...	may ...	Maybe ...
Perhaps ...	might ...	could ...	

10 years from now ...

1 happy?
   I hope I'll be happy.
2 a good job?
   ....
3 good English?
   ....
4 a house?
   ....
5 a millionaire?
   ....
6 married?
   ....
7 children?
   ....
8 abroad?
   ....
9 space travel?
   ....
10 no tooth decay?
   ....
11 another world war?
   ....
12 genetically-engineered babies?
   ....

3.2 Whirlwind European Tours

Keiko, Panos, Walter and Helga are going on a tour of Europe next week. Look at the details of their itinerary.

Monday 7a.m. – flight to Berlin (arrives 8.30a.m.)
Tuesday 8a.m. – flight to Vienna (arrives 9a.m.)
Wednesday 6a.m. – flight to Athens (arrives 8.15a.m.)
Thursday 8a.m. – flight to Rome (arrives 8.15a.m.)
Friday 7a.m. – flight to Geneva (arrives 8.15a.m.)
Saturday 7a.m. – flight to Madrid (arrives 8.45a.m.)
Sunday 7a.m. – flight to Paris (arrives 9a.m.)
Monday 9a.m. – flight to London (arrives 9.45a.m.)

- Accommodation in carefully selected 5-star hotels
- All-day guided bus tour of each city from 11a.m. to 6p.m.
- Lunch in traditional restaurant from 1.30p.m. to 2.30p.m.
- Dinner at hotel from 7p.m. to 8.15p.m.
- Evening entertainment from 8.30p.m.

Using the information above, complete the following sentences with a suitable future form of the verb shown in brackets. The first one has been done as an example.

1 By 10a.m. on Monday, they'll *have arrived* (arrive) in Berlin.
2 At 1.45p.m. on Tuesday, they .... (have) lunch in Vienna.
3 At 6.20a.m. on Wednesday, they...................................... (fly) to Athens.
4 By 8a.m. on Wednesday, they .... (fly) for two hours.
5 By 6p.m. on Thursday, they .... (see) the Colosseum in Rome.

6 By midday on Friday, they .... (tour) Geneva for an hour.
7 At 4 p.m. on Friday, they .... (see) the sights of Geneva.
8 At 7 a.m. on Saturday, they .... (take off) for Madrid.
9 By 2 p.m. on Saturday, they .... (taste) some 'tapas'.
10 By 6 p.m. on Sunday, they .... (go) up the Eiffel Tower in Paris.
11 By 10 p.m. on Sunday, they .... (enjoy) the night-life of Paris.
12 By the time they go to bed on Sunday night, they .... (be) exhausted.
13 By the time they leave for London, they .... (visit) seven different countries in as many days!
14 By the time they get back to London, they .... (take) a lot of photos and they .... (buy) plenty of souvenirs!

4 Phrasal verbs with LET and CUT (Study boxes, pages 96 and 103)

Match up and complete

Find the second half of sentences 1 to 11 in the box below. You will also have to add one or more suitable particles to complete the phrasal verbs with **let** and **cut**. The first one is shown as an example. *as is no. 8*

1 They wouldn't let him in at the club *because he was badly dressed.*
2 The doctor warned her ....
3 Although they cut .... town ....
4 She promised to help us ....
5 The company was prevented from cutting .... the trees ....
6 As it was her first offence, ...
7 One of my jobs on the farm ....
8 The chef cut ..*up*.... the meat into small cubes *before putting it in the pan.*
9 The accident was caused by the taxi driver, ...
10 You have seven days in which to pay your bill, ...
11 Rapunzel let .... her long hair ....

---

was to let .... the chickens every morning at 7 a.m.
but, as usual, she let us .... at the last moment.
after which time your gas supply will be cut ....
to make way for a new supermarket car park.
~~because he was badly dressed.~~
~~before putting it in the pan.~~
she had to cut .... her smoking.
the magistrate let her .... with a suspended sentence.
so that her lover could climb up the tower to her window!
it took them longer than going round the ring-road.
who cut .... in front of the bus and then braked suddenly.

STUDY TIP

PHRASAL VERBS

- A good way of checking/revising phrasal verbs is to see how many you can use with the same particle,

  e.g. <u>up</u> – cut up, set up, break up, get up, put up, etc.

UNIT 6

5 Wordcheck

Technology and gadgets

Fill in the missing words below to reveal the name of another modern invention. One is shown as an example.

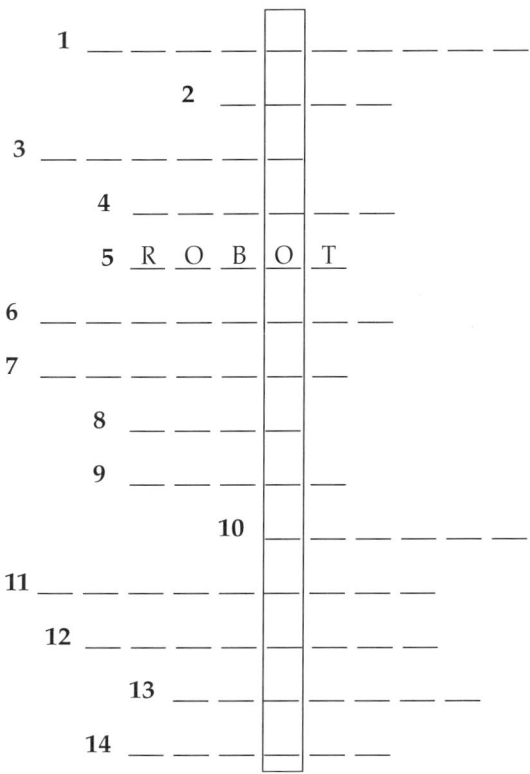

1 Some people now have a satellite dish to watch this. (10)
2 It contains the software needed to use number 6. (4)
3 The part of a modern telephone where you find the numbers to press. (6)
4 The official legal right to make or sell a new invention. (6)
5 A machine made to act and, sometimes, look like a human being. (5)
6 An electronic device for storing and processing information. You might have a 'personal' one. (8)
7 A machine for printing information; used with number 6. (7)
8 Before you speak to someone on the telephone, you must first - - - - the number. (4)
9 A small device you carry or wear which makes a noise if someone wants you to telephone them. (5)
10 Connect a machine to the electricity supply. (4, 2)
11 What you should do when you finish watching TV. (6, 3)
12 This has the letters and symbols necessary for typing. (8)
13 Where you see what you've typed when you use number 6. (7)
14 Where you see the picture in number 1. (6)

6 Grammar round-up

In the following questions complete the second sentence so it has a similar meaning to the first sentence. Use the word given and other words to complete each sentence. You must use between two and five words. Do not change the word given. The first one has been done for you.

1 They took a short cut through the cemetery and arrived before us.
   across
   They cut across the cemetery and arrived before us.
2 Jack has decided to sell his car and walk everywhere.
   is
   Jack .... his car and walk everywhere.
3 He promised not to do it again.
   never
   He said 'I promise I .... again.'
4 By the way, have you got anything definite planned for Saturday?
   are
   By the way, ... anything on Saturday?
5 Bob reduced his intake of fatty food and lost seven kilos in a month!
   on
   Bob .... his intake of fatty food and lost seven kilos in a month!
6 Our exams will be over by this time next month.
   finished
   We .... our exams by this time next month.
7 While mending the road, they accidentally blocked our water pipes.
   cut
   They accidentally .... our water while mending the road.
8 The film starts in five minutes and it'll take us ten minutes to get there.
   already
   By the time we get there, the film .... started.
9 Flight departure time is 10a.m. tomorrow morning.
   off
   The plane .... at 10a.m. tomorrow morning.
10 He felt disappointed when his mother didn't come to see him in the play.
   let
   He felt .... when his mother didn't come to see him in the play.

34

Progress Test Two

UNITS 4–6

Check your progress by entering your score in the box at the end of each exercise and at the end of the complete test.

1 Read the text below and think of the word which best fits each space. Use only **one** word in each space.

Gridlock

(1) .... through the city the other day I got stuck in a traffic jam. The reason for the jam was that the traffic lights were permanently on green and, as a result, the crossroads (2) .... completely blocked. It was two o'clock on a hot July afternoon and I had toothache. I (3) .... to be at the dentist's by three o'clock but I still had an hour so I wasn't (4) .... to start panicking yet.
After half an hour I was still in exactly the same place. Then I saw a traffic warden walking towards me, so I got out and asked him how much longer I'd (5) .... to wait as I had an appointment at three.
'Well,' he said calmly, 'things don't look too good. Three cars have (6) .... down and they can't be moved.'
'So, what can I do?' I asked, with my toothache (7) .... to cause me quite a lot of pain.
'Well, if I (8) .... you, I'd go to the dentist's (9) .... foot.'
'But what (10) .... I do with my car? I can't just abandon it here in the middle of the road. What'll happen if the traffic (11) .... moving again and I'm not here?'
'Well, leave the keys and I (12) .... move it into that parking space over there.'
'But what if someone (13) .... it after you've moved it?' I protested.
'Don't worry, I'll lock it and put the keys in the exhaust pipe.'
Not (14) .... any longer about anything except my toothache, I thanked him and (15) .... off towards the dentist's at a brisk pace. As I walked past the crossroads, I saw the situation was totally out of (16) .... with cars and lorries everywhere. A middle-(17) .... man, whose voice I seemed to recognise, was shouting at another man as the police were trying to make enough space for the breakdown lorry to get (18) .... the three vehicles that couldn't be moved, including a beautiful green Jaguar.
I arrived at the dentist's only five minutes late. The receptionist, (19) .... a little worried, told me that the dentist had been involved in an accident. Apparently someone had reversed into his Jaguar at the traffic lights!
I quickly fixed an appointment for the next day and ran back to the crossroads, which was now clear. I looked down the road and (20) .... out a sigh of relief as I saw my car parked safely on the side of the road.

[20]

2 Read the following text. Look carefully at each line. Some of the lines are correct and some have a word which should not be there. If a line is correct, put a tick (✓) on the dotted line as in the example. If a line has a word which should not be there, write the word on the dotted line as in the example.

The right job for Amanda

Amanda is desperate to get a job. She has left	has.
college over a year ago and still hasn't found	..✓....
anything suitable. 'You needn't to worry.' I	1 ....
tell her, 'you'll find something soon.' 'Unless	2 ....
I will get a job soon, I'll be old enough to retire!	3 ....
I should not to have stayed on at college to get a	4 ....
degree. People think I'm an over-qualified. Look at	5 ....
the people I was at school with – they've all got	6 ....
jobs.' Thinking over what she says, I must have to	7 ....
agree she has a point but I don't think Amanda would	8 ....
be very happy if she had had the sort of job some	9 ....
of her old school friends have.	10 ....

[10]

3 Fill each blank with a suitable form of the word in brackets. See the example provided.

Example: Neil isn't very *interested* (interest) in his job.

1 There's too much traffic .... (congest) in most large towns.
2 He was wearing a loose-.......................... (fit) suit and a big red tie.
3 I soon became familiar with my new .... (surround).
4 There was a .... (hold) at the bank yesterday. They stole about £10,000!
5 We should be there by five, ... (provide) there isn't too much traffic.
6 Soft drink companies should supply their products in .... (reuse) bottles and make people pay a deposit.
7 The computer's OK, but there seems to be something wrong with the .... (print).
8 Some British food is an .... (acquire) taste for foreign visitors.

UNIT 7

9 .... (watch) TV the other night, I happened to see a programme about my home town.
10 The .... (recycle) of what we think of as rubbish will become more and more important over the next 20 years.

[10]

4 Choose the word or phrase which best completes each of the following sentences. Put a circle round the letter you choose as in the example.

Example: I .... I'll pass the exam.
A wish B want C like (D) hope

1 .... I post that letter for you on my way to the office?
A Do B Shall C Would D Will

2 If we all work together, we can get .... the problem somehow.
A away with B round C across D down

3 They set .... the publishing company in 1981.
A in B down C off D up

4 You've got no coke? OK, in that case I .... an orange juice.
A 'll have B 'll having C 'd have D have

5 Jim felt he'd really let his team .... when he missed the penalty.
A out B in C down D off

6 I was terribly nervous so it was a relief that I .... a speech.
A hadn't made B needn't have made
C didn't have to make D mustn't have made

7 You .... look after that car. It might be worth a lot of money one day.
A would B must C should D could

8 He'll never pass his driving test .... he takes some lessons.
A if only B unless C provided D if

9 .... you leave your car outside the library? No, it's a no-parking area.
A Shall B Might C Can D Must

10 A private detective must keep out of .... when following a suspect.
A sight B doors C control D mind

[10]

TOTAL [50]

UNIT 7

1 The definite article (Study box, page 129)

With or without?

Look at the gaps in the following sentences and decide whether to add the definite article (**the**) or not. The first one has been done for you.

1 The Community of Independent States used to be called the USSR.
2 .... Mount Fuji is often seen as a type of symbol for .... Japan.
3 You can go skiing in .... Sierra Nevada in the south of .... Spain.
4 I can never remember if it's .... Nile or .... Amazon which is the longest river in the world.
5 .... Fifth Avenue has some of the most expensive shops in .... New York.
6 Marie has lived on Corsica all her life but she's never seen .... Mediterranean!
7 Most small towns in .... Britain have one main street.
8 Is .... Saudi Arabia part of .... United Arab Emirates?
9 .... Lake Garda is the largest of the Italian lakes.
10 .... Fleet Street in .... London used to be the home of most of the national newspapers produced in .... United Kingdom.

S T U D Y   T I P

THE DEFINITE ARTICLE WITH COUNTRIES AND ISLANDS

- If a country is considered a collection of states or republics, we use the,
  e.g. the UK, the United Arab Emirates, etc.
- Collections of islands also take the,
  e.g. the Bahamas, the Shetlands, etc.
- Singular/large islands do not take the,
  e.g. Madagascar, Sardinia, etc.

2 The gerund (Focus on grammar, pages 134–136)

2.1 Verbs used as nouns

Think of a suitable gerund used as a noun to complete the gaps in these sentences. The first one is shown as an example.

1 It is now generally agreed that *smoking* is one of the principal causes of lung cancer and heart problems.
2 .... is usually the quickest way of getting from one major city to another in the USA.
3 .... is a very popular winter sport in Switzerland and Austria.
4 Many doctors say .... is the best sport for all-round fitness, though it's a good idea to take a few lessons in the local pool first.
5 .... for long periods when you are on holiday can be very harmful, particularly if you've got fair skin.
6 .... your nails is a sign of nervousness and stress.
7 With the ever-increasing use of the telephone, letter-........................... is becoming a dying art.
8 Fox-........................... is still popular in many rural districts of England, though there are more and more opponents to this type of sport.

2.2 Gerunds after prepositions

Make sense of the following sentences by adding a suitable preposition followed by a gerund. The missing prepositions are in bubble **A** and the verbs are in bubble **B**. Look at the first one for an example.

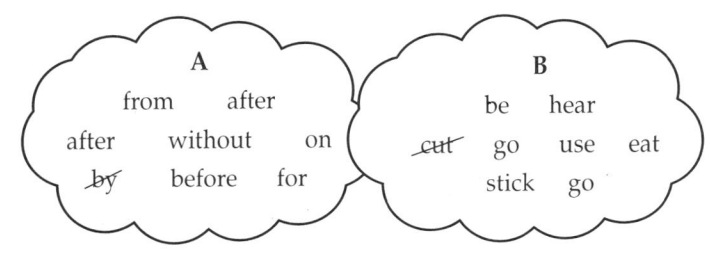

A: from, after, after, without, on, by, before, for

B: be, hear, cut, go, use, eat, stick, go

1 The criminals broke into the computer room *by cutting* a hole in the steel door.
2 .... to bed, I realised I'd left the TV on and had to get up and turn it off.
3 I combed my hair and tried to clean my shoes a bit .... into the boss's office.
4 Isaac Newton worked out the law of gravity .... hit on the head by an apple!
5 Nowadays it's possible to buy almost anything .... cash if you've got a credit card.
6 What's the name of that blue stuff you use .... posters on the wall?
7 .... the news of her win in the lottery, Pam started kissing everybody.
8 Her eating habits got totally out of control when she went .... two or three cakes a day to twenty or more!

2.3 Match up and fill in

Match up the two halves of each sentence and fill in a suitable verb in either the ...ing form or the infinitive. The first one is shown as an example.

1 I'm not used to *getting* much sleep. **E**
2 He avoided .... his military service
3 I wouldn't mind .... rugby again!
4 I really appreciated her .... me at the airport
5 Phil's really looking forward to .... on holiday.
6 She considered .... the police after the burglary
7 The two youths admitted .... the old man's money
8 Martin risked .... arrested
9 Since we moved into the flat I've really missed .... a garden
10 I couldn't stand .... history at school

UNIT 7

A But you said you disliked .... rough games.
B but she decided it wasn't worth .... their time.
C and I still dream about .... the grass on a summer's day.
D when he kept .... anti-government slogans outside the embassy.
E Having a small baby involves *waking up* a lot most nights.
F by .... lies about his age.
G especially as I hadn't asked her to come.
H but I really enjoy .... out about historical facts now.
I He keeps .... us about the beautiful places in Barbados.
J but denied .... him over the head with a stick.

3 Phrasal verbs with BRING (Study box, page 136)

Complete the following sentences with the correct form of a phrasal verb with **bring**. Look at the example in number one.

1 After her parents were killed in a tragic flying accident, she was *brought up* by her grandparents.
2 The government hoped that by devaluing the currency they would .... an economic recovery.
3 I've heard they're going to .... legislation to cut down the amount of pollution caused by car exhaust fumes.
4 Some actors are much better than others at .... the full meaning of what Shakespeare wrote.
5 The doctor had to use smelling salts to .... the boxer .... after he had been knocked out.

4 The past perfect (Focus on grammar, pages 139–140)

An imperfect situation!

Complete the following letters by putting the verbs in brackets in the past perfect simple, the past perfect continuous or the past simple. Look at number one as an example.

22 Bridge Street
Bristol
Friday 10th

Dear Mary,
I'm really sorry I(1) *got* (get) so angry with you last night but I (2) .... (work) for about ten hours when you (3) .... (arrive). I have to admit I (4) .... (forget) we (5) .... (agree) to go out for dinner and I (6) .... (be) in the middle of correcting hundreds of exams. I do hope we'll be able to get together again soon.
With love,

Mick

1 Park Lane
Wells
Saturday 11th

Dear Mick,
Thank you for your letter.
It may surprise you to learn that when we (7) .... *(meet)* last Thursday I (8) .... (work) for the whole day too. Not only that, I (9) .... (be) also very tired as I (10) .... (not go) to bed the night before because of an emergency at the hospital. I'm really sorry, too ... sorry for you. I hadn't realised before your shouting attack just how obsessed you are with your own little world.
As regards getting together, I wouldn't want to come between you and your precious work ever again.
Have a good life.

Mary

5 Verbs of perception (Study box, page 141)

...ing or infinitive?

In the following sentences, decide whether ...ing or the infinitive form is more suitable and cross out the other one. The first one has been done for you.

1 Everyone panicked when they heard the bomb explode/~~exploding~~.
2 As he came downstairs, he heard the children play/playing in the kitchen.
3 As she was walking through the park, she noticed a man throw/throwing a black object into the bushes.
4 We all felt the room move/moving for a second and realised it must have been an earthquake.
5 The kids spent all afternoon watching the workmen cut/cutting down the damaged tree before taking it away on a lorry.
6 Did anyone notice two men sit/sitting in a large green car outside the bank for about two hours yesterday morning?
7 During our week in Turkey, we saw them build/building three more gigantic hotels along the waterfront.
8 We went out in a glass-bottomed boat and watched thousands of incredibly colourful tropical fish swim/swimming in the crystal clear water.
9 I saw the accused throw/throwing a brick through the window, your Honour.

6 Wordcheck

Travel

The name of each of the objects in the pictures is hidden in the box at the top of the next column (vertically, horizontally or diagonally). Find the name and write it out correctly under the corresponding picture. The first one has been done for you.

```
O F I R S T A I D K I T D I B E
S W N E N O L S W A T Z A K R O
N L J P A T G U D C O M P A S S
O N E C O N S L H J A K L E U Q
V O C E P C C I D A Y M X R I S
I S T V P R M O N E Y B E L T O
G O I N I I N P C S D O Z R C V
L U O R Y S N O X K U E N S A U
O V N H F L A G N W L R T I S Z
T E N T P Q L W B V L L A Y E B
O N J I R A M M X A Q A H N K S
H I T C H H I K I N G F E R C T
T R A V E L L E R S C H E Q U E
```

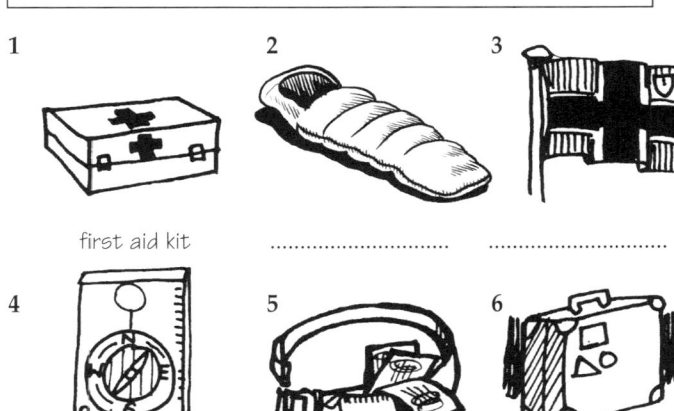

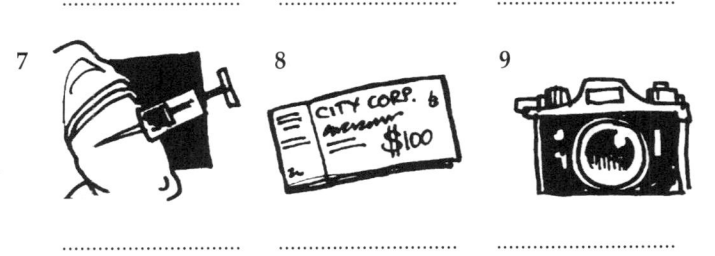

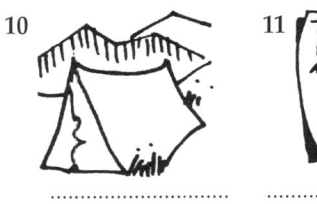

1 first aid kit

UNIT 8

7 Grammar round-up

In the following questions complete the second sentence so it has a similar meaning to the first sentence. Use the word given and other words to complete each sentence. You must use between two and five words. Do not change the word given. The first one has been done for you.

1. Don't worry about your exam too much – there's no point.
   worth
   It *isn't worth worrying* about your exam too much.

2. Stuart mentioned that Nina had phoned the day before.
   Nina's
   Stuart mentioned .... the day before.

3. She won three gold medals before the age of twenty.
   already
   By the age of twenty she .... three gold medals.

4. The cat had hidden itself under my car. Luckily, I noticed before I got in.
   hiding
   Luckily, I .... under my car before I got in.

5. Diana broke that bowl. I saw her do it!
   break
   I saw .... that bowl!

6. He didn't bother to ask for permission to use the phone.
   without
   He used the phone .... permission.

7. Geoff had the accident five hours after he started driving.
   for
   Geoff .... five hours when he had the accident.

8. Hanna has to get up early every morning, which she dislikes intensely.
   objects
   Hanna really .... up early every morning.

9. I don't like the way he shouts at the children.
   his
   I dislike .... at the children.

10. If you want someone to regain consciousness, you should throw cold water in their face.
    bring
    To ...., you should throw cold water in their face.

UNIT 8

1 The infinitive (Focus on grammar, pages 150–152)

1.1 Problems

Look at the following pictures which show some sort of problem and complete the sentences using **too** or **enough** and a suitable adjective and verb from the bubbles. The first one is shown as an example.

Bubble 1: old, deaf, fat, tall, cold, spicy, ~~strong~~, dangerous, fit, poor, dark

Bubble 2: eat, join, buy, swim, play, ~~lift~~, play, drive, hear, fit, drive

1. Wendy isn't *strong enough to lift the box.*

2. Gus is ....

3. Suzy isn't ....

4. The water's ....

5. Sid's ....

6. This food's ....

7 Dick's car ....

8 It's ....

9 Sally's not ....

10 Mrs Knight is ....

11 Chris isn't ....

1.2 The infinitive of purpose

In all of the following sentences, the reason or purpose for doing certain things is missing. Using the verbs and nouns in the bubble below, complete each sentence in a logical way. The first one has been completed for you.

> remember   stress   ~~loan~~
> foreign country   speak   get away from
> improve   save   pollution   time
> overcome   pronunciation   them
> phone   ~~ask for~~   foreign language

1 Joan made an appointment with the bank manager *to ask for a loan.*
2 Why do you write things on the back of your hand? ....!
3 We've decided to move to the countryside ....
4 ...., you first have to dial the international code.
5 We went by taxi ....
6 .... well, you really need to spend some time in the country where it's spoken.
7 Joe has taken up yoga ....
8 Marco and Sybille went to a summer school in England ....

STUDY TIP

INFINITIVE OF PURPOSE (why you do things)
• Make a special note of this form. Many languages express purpose differently (usually with the equivalent of <u>for</u>!)

1.3 With or without

In the following sentences there is a gap before each infinitive. Decide whether to add **to** or not. The first one has been done as an example.

1 You really ought <u>to</u> do the washing-up more often – this place is a mess!
2 I know I shouldn't .... bite my nails, but I'm very nervy.
3 I'd love .... go to the Bahamas. Would you? I'd prefer .... go to Indonesia.
4 The police didn't allow me .... take any photographs of the accident. However, they let me .... interview some of the witnesses.
5 Why not .... come round for supper tomorrow evening?
6 Would you like .... bring that delightful sister of yours?
7 You don't have .... understand every word to get the general idea.
8 You mustn't .... panic if you don't understand some words.
9 When I was a kid, my grandfather would .... tell me stories about life in India.
10 I used .... suck my thumb all the time and I didn't stop until I was 10!
11 The customs official made Sandra .... open all her baggage.
12 She was made .... pay a fine for importing too many cigarettes.
13 We'd better .... stop now before we get too confused!

UNIT 8

2 Phrasal verbs with LOOK (Study box, page 152)

If looks could kill ...

Complete the following sentences with a suitable form of a phrasal verb with **look** and any other necessary information. The first one has been done for you.

1. When a serious crime is committed, the police have to look into it.
2. If you don't know some of the words, you can ....
3. Jan's very sociable. Whenever she passes the house she always ....
4. A nanny is someone who is responsible for ....
5. When she went to the police station to identify the criminal, they gave her hundreds of photos to ....
6. She always .... her elder sister who was a talented musician.
7. If you're planning on walking round the city after dark, ...!
8. There are still some prospectors who go to the Yukon .... gold.

3 Reporting statements (Focus on grammar, pages 156–57)

3.1 But they promised ...!

Look at the statements made by the leader of the government *before* the election and then read the newspaper headlines which show what happened *after* his party was re-elected. React to the headlines as you think a voter would react. The first one is shown as an example.

1. You will NOT have to pay so much tax!
2. We GUARANTEE there will be no increase in the cost of using public transport.
3. We are making great progress in cutting down pollution in our cities.
4. Old age pensions will go up by at least 10%!
5. We are going to provide more hospital services in every city.
6. We have signed agreements with 20 international companies to set up here and bring more jobs.
7. We have ALREADY started employment training programmes for school leavers.
8. We PROMISE to clean up all rivers and beaches.

1 GOVERNMENT INCREASES TAX TO 25 PER CENT

2 TRAIN FARE SHOCK – prices go up 10 per cent

3 CITY SMOG THE WORST FOR 40 YEARS!

4 *No increase in pensions this year*

5 NATIONAL HEALTH SCANDAL 10 more hospitals close

6 Government fails to attract international companies

7 GOVERNMENT ADMITS NO MONEY FOR YOUTH TRAINING SCHEMES

8 10 MORE BEACHES FAIL EUROPEAN STANDARDS OF CLEANLINESS!!!

1. But they told us *we wouldn't have to pay so much tax!*
2. But they guaranteed ....
3. But they said ....
4. But they ....
5. But ....
6. ....
7. ....
8. ....

3.2 Or words to that effect

Put the following sentences into reported speech and choose a suitable reporting verb. See the example provided in number one.

1 'Yes, OK, it was me who broke the window.'
   Jenny *admitted that she had broken the window.*
2 'Why don't you go to Scotland for your holidays?'
   Duncan ....
3 'Don't worry. I'll never tell anyone about your secret!'
   Liza's friend ....
4 'Whatever you do, don't walk around the port after dark, it can be very dangerous.'
   Clint ....
5 'Would you like to come round for a coffee?'
   Angela ....
6 'The car won't start because you've flooded the engine with petrol.'
   The mechanic ....
7 'I'm not really learning anything with this method of teaching.'
   One of her students ....
8 'Can you put your toys away before you go to bed, kids?'
   The children's mother ....
9 'I shouldn't drink the tap water if I were you.'
   The tour guide ....
10 'Be careful – the castle is haunted!'
   The old gardener ....

3.3 His actual words were ...

The following sentences are all reported statements. Write what you think each person actually said in each case. A suggested answer is given for number one.

1 The doctor warned him that he would have a heart attack unless he cut down on fried food.

   'Look! You'll have a heart attack unless you cut down on fried food!'

2 The lawyer argued that his client couldn't have committed the murder as he had been seen 10 miles away at the time.
   '..,
   ....'

3 The receptionist reminded me to hand in my key before I left.
   '..,
   ....'
4 Their father forbade them to speak unless they were spoken to.
   '..
   ....'
5 The representative reminded the secretary that the company still hadn't paid for the last consignment of goods.
   '..
   ....'
6 Paco recommended them to eat a strong local sausage called 'chorizo'.
   '..
   ....'
7 We asked them not to throw litter in our garden.
   '..
   ....'
8 The policeman told us not to worry and promised to investigate the matter.
   '..
   ....'
9 The man sitting next to us told us to keep our tickets in case an inspector got on.
   '..
   ....'
10 The psychiatrist suggested he should start by talking about his earliest memories.
   '..
   ....'

4 Phrasal verbs with GET (Study box, page 158)

In other words

Replace the words or phrases in darker print in the following sentences with a suitable form of a phrasal verb with **get**. The first is shown as an example.

UNIT 8

1 When she realised she was on the wrong bus, she **left**/ got off.
2 I can never **find time to repair**/ .... the bathroom tap.
3 Molly isn't **making good progress**/ .... at her new school.
4 Mr McQueen has never really **recovered from**/ .... the shock of his wife's death.
5 After several attempts, she eventually managed to **reach**/ .... him on his car phone.
6 Roy changed his job because he couldn't **manage to work with**/ .... his boss.
7 Paul always uses that excuse about his bad back to **avoid**/ .... doing any gardening.

5 Comparatives (Focus on grammar, page 160)

The bigger they come, the harder they fall.

Use the following skeleton sentences to create full sentences to show the relationship between the words given. Look at the example in number one.

1 old/chicken/tough
   The older the chicken, the tougher it is to eat.
2 careful/student/mistakes
   ....
   ....
3 perfect/diamond/expensive
   ....
   ....
4 ripe/plums/sweet
   ....
   ....
5 cold/weather/chance of snow
   ....
   ....
6 coffee/Richard/nervous
   ....
   ....
7 quickly/someone eat/chance of indigestion
   ....
   ....
8 close to centre/house/rent
   ....
   ....

6 Definite article or not? (Study box, page 161)

Decide whether or not to add the definite article in the gaps in the following sentences. The first one has been done for you.

1 June was so tired yesterday afternoon that she went to ......—......... bed at 5 o'clock!
2 We visited .... church to take some photos of the famous mosaics.
3 Donald is studying law at .... university.
4 Mary only goes to .... church for christenings, weddings and funerals.
5 We sometimes take our students to .... court so they can see how British justice works.
6 Sammy went over to .... bed to find his pyjamas.
7 Mrs Walton works as a part-time secretary at .... school.
8 Two detectives went to .... college to interview the principal.
9 They're building a new library at .... university.
10 They got so fed up with their neighbour's loud parties that they took him to .... court.
11 Mark had to go to .... hospital for tests.
12 Tony is going to .... prison next week to give some talks on bird-watching.

S T U D Y   T I P
• • • • • • • • • • • • • • • • • •
THE DEFINITE ARTICLE

• We DON'T use the definite article with the group of words above if we are talking about the 'primary function' of the word,
e.g. the primary function
of a <u>prison</u> is to hold and punish criminals;
of a <u>hospital</u>, to treat the sick and injured;
of a <u>church</u>, to provide a place of worship.

---

7 Wordcheck

Home life

Complete the missing words in the following sentences. The first one is shown as an example.

1 Although Helen is a *single parent* and has nobody to help her look after the children, she never complains and always seems full of life!

2 Sean is an o.................. c..................; he often wishes he had a brother or sister.
3 When I was a child, my parents gave me a little p.................. m.................. every week to spend on records, sweets and occasional visits to the cinema.
4 Maria is divorced but often sees her e.................. -h.................. as they work for the same company!
5 I hate doing most h.................. c.................., particularly ironing and washing-up.
6 In my grandfather's day, men were never expected to help with the h.................. .
7 They live in an amazing house full of the latest gadgets and m.................. c.................. .
8 Sylvia has a well-paid job and contributes much more to the f.................. b.................. than her husband, Toby.
9 Older women find it hard to give up their c.................. to have children.
10 There are a lot of advantages to g.................. u.................. with several brothers and sisters.

8 Grammar round-up

In the following questions complete the second sentence so it has a similar meaning to the first sentence. Use the word given and other words to complete each sentence. You must use between two and five words. Do not change the word given. The first one has been done for you.

1 'Hey Jim, don't forget to switch off the lights when you leave,' Miriam said.
reminded
Miriam *reminded Jim to switch off* the lights when he left.
2 You pay more if the package weighs more.
heavier
The .... the more you pay.
3 'Your flight may be delayed,' she said.
that
She told .... be delayed.
4 Jane has always had great respect for her grandfather.
looked
Jane has always .... her grandfather.
5 I can't get my desk in this room, it's too small.
big
This room .... to get my desk in.
6 Jack arrives home late so that he doesn't have to go shopping.
gets
Jack .... shopping by arriving home late.

7 Sid reminded us to take an umbrella in case it rained.
forget
Sid said, '.. an umbrella in case it rains.'
8 Suzy couldn't reach the picture without a ladder.
for
The picture was too high up .... without a ladder.
9 The police forced the demonstrators to leave the factory.
made
The police .... the factory.
10 Amy wanted a fresh start in life, so she emigrated to New Zealand.
order
Amy emigrated to New Zealand .... a fresh start in life.

UNIT 9

1 Expressing quantity (Focus on grammar, pages 167–168)

1.1 *Right or wrong?*

Decide if the following sentences are right or wrong. If a sentence is wrong, write a possible correction for it. The first one is shown as an example.

1 It was such a̶ terrible weather that we stayed inside and played cards.
2 Good morning. I'd like an information about the old city, please.
3 This spaghetti tastes a little over-cooked, doesn't it?
4 We've booked to go on a travel to Australia.
5 It's important to take plenty of exercise if you want to stay fit.
6 The police found some blood in the car but no fingerprints.
7 Lord and Lady Notlaw live in an old country house full of the most beautiful antique furnitures.
8 I feel really sorry for them. They haven't got a single money.
9 People keep telling me that my hairs are turning grey.
10 Mrs Cram is very depressed a lot of the times.
11 He didn't like the baby so much after she pulled out some of the hairs on his forearm!
12 The news about the political situation were rather worrying.

UNIT 9

> **STUDY TIP**
>
> **COUNTABLE AND UNCOUNTABLE NOUNS**
> - Many words which in English are surprisingly seen as uncountable may be seen as countable in other languages,
> e.g. hair, money.
> - Make a careful note of those which are different in your language.

1.2 You can't say that.

Decide which of the alternatives provided (A, B or C) is **not** possible in each of the following sentences and cross it out. An example is shown in number one.

1. They say Mr Lamb keeps .... money in his mattress.
   A a great deal of B a lot of C ~~a great~~ many
2. We can't all sit down, there are .... chairs.
   A too little B too few C not enough
3. Gerald can't go on holiday this year as he's got .... time off.
   A very little B hardly any C too few
4. A car of this size requires .... parking space.
   A plenty of B a great many C a lot of
5. .... football fans were arrested after the match.
   A A great deal of B Very many C A large number of
6. Her questions showed .... sensitivity.
   A a lack of B too few C too little
7. Timmy ate .... cream and felt sick.
   A too much B a large number of C a large amount of
8. I'm afraid there's .... understanding between the strikers and the management.
   A too few B a lack of C hardly any
9. Newspaper editors don't like the summer months as there is often .... news to fill up their papers with.
   A very little B too few C a lack of
10. .... tourists get sunburnt on their first day at the beach.
    A A great many B A great deal of C A lot of

2 Verbs and prepositions (Study box, page 171)

Got a match?

Match beginnings of sentences in column A with endings in column B. The first has been done for you.

A

1. We all accused Jake — H
2. Let me congratulate you
3. I quickly apologised
4. Haggis consists
5. Judy spent an hour arguing with the other driver
6. None of the witnesses could provide the detectives
7. I always confuse Robert
8. Turn that TV down! How can I concentrate
9. The climbers were discouraged
10. Alf spends all his spare cash
11. Babs has just applied
12. Many students find it difficult to distinguish
13. Ben almost always disagrees
14. Mr and Mrs Stanley have surrounded their garden
15. The police had to protect their key witness

B

A from making the ascent in the fog.
B on my homework?
C with his twin brother, Stephen.
D on new programs for his computer.
E with a high fence to stop people looking at them from the bus.
F with his flatmate about whose turn it is to do the washing-up.
G from a probable murder attempt.
H of lying but he was telling the truth.
I on your promotion to manager.
J for asking such a stupid question.
K between 'bring' and 'take'!
L bits of meat and oatmeal cooked inside a sheep's stomach!
M about whose fault the accident was.
N with a clear description of the bank robber.
O for the post of manageress at the supermarket.

STUDY TIP

VERBS AND PREPOSITIONS

- Note particularly those verbs which take different or no prepositions in your own language.
- Group verbs with the same preposition, e.g. depend on, congratulate on, etc.; apologise for, wait for, etc.

3 Reported questions (Focus on grammar, pages 171–172)

3.1 Just a few questions ...

Last week, Sid was stopped by a market researcher and asked some questions. Read through them below.

How often do you buy new clothes?
When did you last buy an article of clothing?
Where do you usually buy your clothes?
What's the most you've ever spent on one article?
When are you next going to buy some clothes?
Have you ever visited Lennon's Fashion House?
Would you like a Lennon's credit card?
Can I show you round Lennon's for 5 minutes?

Three hours later Sid arrived back home. Complete the conversation he had with Doris, his wife. The first gap has been completed for you.

Sid: Hello, dear. I'm sorry I'm late, but I was stopped by a market researcher.
Doris: Oh really! What happened?
Sid: Well, she just wanted to ask me some questions.
Doris: Oh yes? What did she ask you?
Sid: Well, first she asked me how often (1) *I bought new clothes.*
Doris: Yes.
Sid: Then she wanted to know when (2) ....
Doris: Go on.
Sid: After that she asked me where (3) .... and what (4) ....
Doris: Oh dear!
Sid: Next she wanted to know when (5) .... and if (6) ....
Doris: Oh no. That's that expensive new shop.
Sid: Finally she asked me if (7) .... and if (8) ....
Doris: And you of course said yes. How much have you spent?
Sid: How should I know? I used my new credit card.

3.2 Making a good impression

The phrases below are used to show politeness or delicateness when asking questions. First, put the phrases in order of politeness with the most polite first. Then use an appropriate phrase to form polite questions from the prompts given. An example is provided in both cases.

1. Do you know ...   ☐
2. I wonder if you could tell me ...   ☐
3. Could you possibly tell me ...   ☐
4. I wonder if you could possibly tell me ...   1
5. Do you happen to know ...   ☐
6. Can you tell me ...   ☐

A   what 'swot'?

Do you know what 'swot' means?

B   if

....

C   how much ....?

D   how old ....?

E   why ....?

F   which ....?

G   what time ....?

H   where ....?

4 Expressing number (Focus on grammar, pages 175–176)

Complete the following sentences using the words in the box below. The first one has been done for you.

both	each	every	either	neither	either
all	none	~~both~~	all	none	

1   His grandfather was partially blinded in *both* eyes during the war.
2   Although Eric and Martin were .... born in Verona, ... of them speaks a word of Italian.
3   There are two roads that lead to the beach but I wouldn't advise you to drive down .... of them!
4   Can you lend me some money? Why? Because I've got .... !
5   Tracey had five pens in her bag but .... of them worked.
6   At the exhibition we saw a big glass prism that splits up .... the colours of the rainbow – it was really beautiful.
7   Charlie, Gill and Wendy .... have different plans. .... thinks theirs is the best and won't even consider .... of the other plans.
8   Nigel has read .... book ever written by Dickens.

5 Phrasal verbs with COME (Study box, page 177)

Each of the sentences in column A has two different endings in column B. Match up the beginnings with the different endings. An example is provided in number one.

A

1   The apple blossom   [D] [G]
2   Douglas came across   [ ] [ ]
3   The injured woman   [ ] [ ]
4   I do hope   [ ] [ ]
5   We thought we were going the right way   [ ] [ ]

B

A   when we came up against a dead end.
B   came to when the doctor put her head between her legs.
C   this scheme to redevelop the old port will come off.
D   came up against some extremely hard frosts and was killed off.
E   when we came across a signpost we'd passed 10 minutes before!
F   as an extremely competent sales manager at the meeting.
G   comes out earlier in the south west of the country.
H   is still in a coma, though the doctors say she'll come round sooner or later.

I some old letters while clearing out the attic.
J you'll be able to come round on Friday evening.

6 Wordcheck – health, illness and treatment

6.1 Word groups

Sort the words in the box below into eight word groups. Each group has three words. Provide a name for each group. See the example given.

```
        graze   blistering   apply    fibre
butter  antiseptic  carbohydrates  bandage  protein
treat   aspirin   bruise   flu   milk   cold   cheese
fever   compress   scratch   relieve   injection
             plaster   burn   scab
```

	butter	cheese	milk		dairy products
1	....	....	....	=	....
2	....	....	....	=	....
3	....	....	....	=	....
4	....	....	....	=	....
5	....	....	....	=	....
6	....	....	....	=	....
7	....	....	....	=	....
8	....	....	....	=	....

6.2 Word partners

Match each word in column A with its partner in column B. The first one is shown as an example.

#	A		B
1	dairy	C	A tooth
2	digestive		B solution
3	antiseptic		C products
4	blood		D pills
5	soluble		E system
6	tetanus		F pressure
7	sweet		G aspirin
8	vitamin		H injection

7 Grammar round-up

In the following questions complete the second sentence so it has a similar meaning to the first sentence. Use the word given and other words to complete each sentence. You must use between two and five words. Do not change the word given. The first one has been done for you.

1 Stephanie realised she shouldn't have laughed and said 'Sorry'.
   apologised
   Stephanie *apologised for laughing.*

2 There's very little petrol in the car.
   hardly
   There's .... in the car.

3 'Have you ever considered a complete change of career?' she asked me.
   if
   She wanted to know .... a complete change of career.

4 The developers were faced with serious problems when they tried to build the supermarket near the park.
   came
   The developers .... serious problems when they tried to build the supermarket near the park.

5 All the children were given a toy car at the end of the visit.
   each
   At the end of the visit .... given a toy car.

6 The headmaster advised Steve not to study physics.
   discouraged
   The headmaster .... physics.

7 A great many murder cases are never solved.
   large
   A .... murder cases are never solved.

8 Percival happened to find a valuable old painting in a junk shop.
   came
   Percival .... a valuable old painting in a junk shop.

9 There wasn't enough interest in the plan.
   lack
   There .... interest in the plan.

10 The policeman asked her where she had been the previous evening.
   last
   'Where .... ?'
   The policeman asked her.

PROGRESS TEST THREE

Progress Test Three

UNITS 6–9

Check your progress by entering your score in the box at the end of each exercise and at the end of the complete test.

1 Read the text below and think of the word which best fits each space. Use only **one** word in each space.

Holiday Adventure
About five years ago a friend and I went on a cheap camping holiday to the Greek islands. One day we arrived on the island of Paxos as we wanted to go to (1) ……………… church in the main town (2) ……………… take some photographs of its famous mosaics. After (3) ……………… the mosaics we walked down to the beach, which, we discovered, was absolutely full of tourists. We'd been (4) ……………… on the beach for 20 minutes when we decided we were fed up with being surrounded by so many people and my friend went and asked a young man if there (5) ……………… any less crowded beaches nearby. He said there was a beautiful beach about five kilometres up the coast and that (6) ……………… any tourists went there as it was too far from the hotels and bars! He explained that we would have to (7) ……………… for a white signpost with the name of a villa written on it and the beach was just off the road on the right. We thanked him and started walking up the road. After some time we (8) ……………… across a yellow signpost saying Villa Magus. We wondered if it was the right place as the young man (9) ……………… said it was a white signpost. Then we looked down to our right and could just see someone (10) ……………… on a deserted sandy beach far below. We decided that this was the place for us. (11) ……………… get to the beach, we had to climb down a steep hill covered in trees. Halfway down the hill we came (12) ……………… against a high stone wall in the middle of the wood. I climbed over first and my friend threw over our rucksacks. Then he started climbing over. However, while (13) ……………… down on my side of the wall, he fell to the ground, hit his head and passed out. I immediately tried to (14) ……………… him round by throwing cold water on his face but he didn't move. Then suddenly I heard a noise. I turned round and saw an enormous dog (15) ……………… at me with big black eyes. I just froze. After what seemed like ages a young woman appeared and asked me (16) ……………… I knew I was on private property. I (17) ……………… for climbing over her wall and explained what had (18) ……………… to my friend. Ten minutes later we were in her villa and my friend had come round. The woman told us she was actually quite happy we had 'dropped in' as there was a terrible (19) ……………… of people to talk to! She invited us to put up our (20) ……………… in her garden and we stayed for two glorious weeks, eating in the villa and sunbathing on her private beach.

[20]

2 Fill each blank with a suitable form of the word in brackets. See the example provided.

Example: Neil isn't very *interested* (interest) in his job.

1 They're always having arguments because he totally ……………… (agree) with her ideas on how to bring up children.
2 The doctor put a sterile ……………… (dress) on the cut on my leg.
3 When we were children we always helped our mother with the ……………… (house) chores.
4 Chris is terribly ……………… (health) because he never takes any exercise and he smokes like a chimney!
5 Experts say that your ……………… (bring) has a great influence on your eating habits as an adult.
6 He grew up in a tough ……………… (neighbour). Maybe that's why he became a professional boxer.
7 ……………… (accommodate) is very expensive in the centre of the city.
8 It's important to use reliable ……………… (equip) when you go mountaineering.
9 They were ……………… (courage) from attempting the journey through the desert to the oasis without a local guide.
10 My father always told me to eat my food in small ……………… (mouth) and to chew it 33 times!

[10]

3 Read the following text. Look carefully at each line. Some of the lines are correct and some have a word which should not be there. If a line is correct, put a tick (✓) on the dotted line as in the examples. If a line has a word which should not be there, write the word on the dotted line as in the example.

Away from it all

Last July three friends and I decided to rent a holiday cottage in the Cornwall. I telephoned a company called Cornish Chalets and the woman said she had thought she had a place although it was a bit isolated. I said, 'Fine, the quieter the better.' Before we moved in, we met the owner of the cottage who gave us the key and some instructions on how using the generator! As we drove far away, I saw him smiling and shaking his head. When we opened the door of the cottage, I understood why. We saw a big rat to run right across the floor. There was so much of damp that the walls were green! Some holiday!

..✓..
the
1 ....
2 ....
3 ....
4 ....
5 ....
6 ....
7 ....
8 ....
9 ....
10 ....

10

4 Choose the word or phrase which best completes each of the following sentences. Put a circle round the letter you choose, as in the example.

Example: I .... I'll pass the exam.
A wish   B want   C like   (D) hope

1 If you're looking for a job, you'll need a work ....
  A licence   B permit   C pass   D card

2 Demy phoned to congratulate me .... passing my driving test.
  A on   B for   C with   D in

3 When going on long journeys abroad, I always take plenty of .... parts for my motorbike.
  A extra   B free   C additional   D spare

4 My grandfather had a hard .... – he was sent out to work when he was ten.
  A growing   B career   C childhood   D education

5 It's no .... talking to Andy when he's reading. He'll just ignore you.
  A good   B point   C result   D worth

6 If you want to help, perhaps you could .... the table for dinner.
  A put   B lay   C spread   D place

7 Joe thinks we've invited too many guests, but I say the more the .... !
  A nicer   B happier   C merrier   D greater

8 No more washing dirty plates for us. We've bought a new .... !
  A vacuum cleaner   B washing machine
  C dishwasher   D spin-drier

9 You must put a .... under your sleeping bags or you'll get wet!
  A sleeping sheet   B tent sheet
  C dust sheet   D ground sheet

10 I always do the housework on Saturday as I can never get .... it during the week.
  A out of   B over   C round to   D off

10

TOTAL   50

UNIT 10

1 Expressing time (Focus on grammar, pages 182–183)

Holiday romance

Complete the following passage with suitable time expressions from the box below. The first one is shown as an example.

first	previously	during	by the time
later	before	then	after	as soon as
meanwhile	while	when	until	during

This was Sarah's first trip to Italy for fifteen years. She had (1) *previously* been there as a child and now she was going for a whole year!
(2) .... catching the train at Victoria Station, she bought a Teach-Yourself-Italian book to study (3) .... the long journey. She got on the train and sat down in an empty compartment. But as it happened, she didn't have time to do much studying. (4) .... a rather attractive young man came into the compartment and started chatting to her (5) .... he sat down. (6) .... in came a mother and two noisy little children who, (7) .... their mother was getting the rest of their luggage, started jumping on the seats and falling all over Sarah and the young man. (8) .... their mother came back, she started shouting at the children. But the children took very little notice of her and carried on with their rough games.
(9) .... the young man had introduced himself as Luca and had invited Sarah to come and stay with him in Bologna (10) .... she could

find a flat to rent. Sarah decided to put her book away and maybe study it later (11) .... they had crossed the Channel and arrived in France. But Luca just kept talking (12) .... the Channel crossing and for the rest of the journey. (13) .... they arrived in Bologna they were both very tired but happy.
It's now five years (14) .... Luca and Sarah got married two years ago and have two noisy little children of their own.

2 Purpose clauses (Study box, page 188)

Why, oh why?

Finish each of the following sentences by combining words from bubble A with words from bubble B, as in the example.

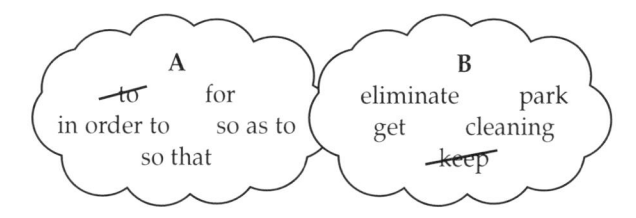

```
        A                         B
   to     for            eliminate      park
in order to  so as to        get      cleaning
     so that                    keep
```

1 I don't understand why you've covered the sofa with that sheet.
  To keep it clean when they're sweeping the chimney.
2 What do you use that old shirt for?
  .... the windows with.
3 Why do the police want to take my fingerprints? I'm not a suspect.
  .... you from their inquiries, that's all.
4 What's the point in my getting a permit for the car?
  .... you can .... outside your office in the city centre.
5 Why is Erica climbing up that tree?
  .... a better view of the parade.

STUDY TIP

TO + INFINITIVE VS. FOR + ...ING

- When saying the reason why, use only <u>to</u> + infinitive,
  e.g. I braked <u>to</u> avoid (not: for avoiding) the dog.
- When describing the use made of something, both forms are possible,
  e.g. A thermometer is an instrument
        <u>for</u> measuring temperature with;
        <u>to</u> measure temperature with.

3 Phrasal verbs with GO (Study box, page 193)

Go for it!

Find and correct the mistakes made with the use of the phrasal verbs in the sentences below. The first one has been done for you.

1 This cheese looks a bit green. I think it's gone ~~over~~ *off*.
2 While she was on holiday, Louise went in for a bad case of food poisoning.
3 Why don't you buy the green shirt? It would go on your eyes.
4 The customs official went with the contents of my suitcases very carefully.
5 Carol has decided not to go down with that silly beauty contest after all.
6 Norman found an old hand grenade in the wood. Luckily, it didn't go on.
7 Betty missed the last bus home as the lecture went off until 10.30 p.m.
8 The policeman went on the two statements carefully to see if there were any disagreements.
9 Many young doctors go through sleep for up to 48 hours. This can lead to serious mistakes owing to fatigue.
10 If you really want to know what's going off in the world, you should buy a decent newspaper!

4 Modal verbs: certainty, probability and possibility (Focus on grammar, pages 188–189)

Are you sure?

Complete the following sentences with a verb form expressing certainty, probability or possibility and another verb which fits into the context in a logical way. Look at the example in number one.

1. There's someone at the door.
   It *must be* the postman, he always comes at this time.
2. Why didn't Pat phone you back?
   I suppose he .... the message I left for him.
3. Do you think it's a dog?
   No, it .... , it's far too big. Let's run!
4. Sandra was using the dictionary earlier.
   She .... where it is.
5. Do you think I should take an umbrella?
   It looks fine to me, but I suppose it .... later on.
6. With all the doors and windows locked it's hard to see how anyone .... the diamonds. But they did.
7. .... you .... your wallet in the changing room, do you think?
8. Acupuncture .... people with a lot of different problems, including giving up smoking.
9. Look at the time, they're over an hour late now!
   Yes, they .... completely .... about the meeting.
10. He always left the TV switched on. .... that .... the fire?
11. But you were at home when the burglary took place. You .... them break the window.
12. I wouldn't eat those mushrooms if I were you. I think they .... poisonous.

STUDY TIP

CAN VS. MAY, MIGHT, COULD

- <u>can</u> is not used when making a deduction about something,

  e.g. What's that? I think it ~~can~~ be a fish. *may/might/could*

---

5 Prepositional phrases (Study box, page 192)

In doubt ...

Substitute the words in italics in the following sentences with a prepositional phrase that means the same thing. The first one is shown as an example.

1. Could you come here *immediately*/ at once?
2. I'm sorry. I broke it *accidentally*/ ....
3. When the fire brigade arrived, the house had been *burning*/ .... for more than half an hour.
4. *At the beginning*/ .... I thought she was rather sarcastic but now I quite like her.
5. We only realised after we had been rescued that our lives had been *threatened*/ ....
6. Depress the clutch while, *simultaneously*/ .... , moving the gear into second.
7. *Occasionally*/ .... I wonder if my brother is a little mad.
8. Thank goodness you're here *finally*/ .... I thought you'd got lost.
9. It was a serious operation but she's *safe*/ .... now.
10. We called eight restaurants but they were all fully booked. So, *after all this*/ .... , we decided to stay at home.
11. You seem to be *having some trouble*/ .... Would you like me to give you a push?

6 Question tags (Focus on grammar, pages 192–193)

It's right, isn't it?

Decide if the question tags in the following sentences are used correctly. Correct any mistakes you find as in the example in number one.

1. Muriel's got two sons, ~~doesn't~~ *hasn't* she?
2. You can't cook very well, can you?

UNIT 10

3 She had a red car last time, hadn't she?
4 He spoke very quickly, didn't he?
5 Someone must have forgotten to lock the door, mustn't they?
6 Don't tell anyone about this, would you?
7 You'd better take an aspirin, wouldn't you?
8 Greg's got no time for relaxation anymore, hasn't he?
9 Nothing's going to stop us now, is it?
10 They'd rather be at home, wouldn't they?
11 Oh, just shut up for a moment, don't you?
12 I'm in the right office, amn't I?
13 We haven't met before, have we?
14 Nobody here can speak Russian, can't they?
15 We'd been there before, didn't we?

STUDY TIP

QUESTION TAGS AND INTONATION

- The correct intonation is as important as the correct form for question tags.
  - falling intonation (common) in the question tag invites agreement.
  - rising intonation (less common) in the question tag asks a genuine question.

7 Wordcheck

Danger, escape and reactions

In each of the following groups of words there is one that doesn't fit. Underline the odd word out. The first one has been done for you.

1 horrific	terrifying	<u>mystified</u>	disastrous
2 weeping	sobbing	crying	shaking
3 explosion	decompression	blaze	crash
4 gasp	fracture	wound	frostbite
5 fall	leap	shatter	dive
6 smoulder	burn	thud	flame
7 jinxed	glad	unhurt	lucky
8 screaming	limping	shouting	gasping
9 alertness	shock	panic	anxiety
10 snatch	grab	grip	tangle

8 Grammar round-up

In the following questions complete the second sentence so it has a similar meaning to the first sentence. Use the word given and other words to complete each sentence. You must use between two and five words. Do not change the word given. The first one has been done for you.

1 Eating no food for long periods is not a good idea!
   without
   It's not a good idea *to go without* food for long periods.

2 Immediately the admiral steps off the ship, we must all salute.
   soon
   We must all salute ....
   the admiral steps off the ship.

3 She took her shoes off in order not to make any noise.
   so
   She took her shoes off ....
   .... any noise.

4 Ask Malcolm. Perhaps he took your pen by mistake.
   might
   Ask Malcolm. He ....
   your pen by mistake.

5 Kitty will surely fail her exam, won't she?
   chance
   Kitty .... of passing her exam, has she?

6 Did you visit the pyramids while you were staying in Cairo?
   during
   Did you visit the pyramids ....
   in Cairo?

7 Those eggs will be rotten by now.
   off
   Those eggs ....
   by now.

8 The only possible explanation is that the fire was started deliberately.
   must
   The fire ....
   deliberately.

9 We should report this, shouldn't we?
   better
   We'd ....
   we?

10 I didn't mean to wake the baby when I rang your bell.
   accident
   I ....
   when I rang your bell.

UNIT 11

1 The passive voice (Focus on grammar, pages 198–199)

1.1 What do you know?

Complete the sentences below by adding a suitable verb in the passive voice. (If you need any help, look at the box after the exercise.) The first one has been done for you.

1 Penicillin *was discovered by Fleming.*
2 Honey ....
3 The radio ....
4 The song 'Yesterday' ....
5 The *Titanic* ....
6 Italian pasta ....
7 'Psycho' ....
8 Beer ....
9 Napoleon Bonaparte ....
10 America ....
11 The Opera 'La Traviata' ....
12 Pelota ....
13 Silk ....
14 Pompeii ....
15 The 'Walkman' ....

flour and eggs	Marconi	worms	an iceberg
bees	Verdi	Sony	hops and barley
a volcanic eruption	Waterloo	Hitchcock
the Beatles	~~Fleming~~	Spain	Columbus

1.2 Headlines and notices

Expand the following headlines and notices into more complete English. The first one is shown as an example.

MISSING GIRL FOUND SAFE

NO VEHICLES BEYOND THIS POINT

ARREST IMMINENT FOR MAFIA BOSS

Cheques accepted with guarantee card only

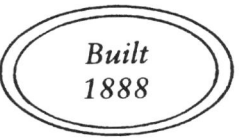

Built 1888

SPORTS STADIUM TO BE OPENED BY PRINCESS ON SATURDAY

Valuable earring lost here
Sat 4th — reward offered.
Tel: 432775

PROMOTION LIKELY FOR LOCAL BBC CHIEF

BREAKTHROUGH IN TREATMENT OF CANCER

No unaccompanied children in lift

1 A missing girl *has been found safe.*
2 Vehicles ....
3 A Mafia boss ....
4 Cheques ....
5 Our house ....
6 The new sports stadium ....
7 A valuable earring ....
8 A local BBC chief ....
9 A breakthrough ....
10 Children ....

1.3 Stating the obvious

In the following sentences the subject is either not important or too obvious to be necessary. Change each sentence into a more natural passive sentence, as in the example in number one.

1. The cleaners were cleaning the room when I arrived.
   The room was being cleaned when I arrived.
2. Thieves have stolen a priceless antique vase from the British Museum.
   ....
   ....
3. Nobody should have opened this letter. It's private.
   ....
   ....
4. The printers accidentally printed the cover of the book upside-down.
   ....
   ....
5. The actors are going to perform the play outdoors.
   ....
   ....
6. Some people are using the lecture hall next Friday.
   ....
   ....
7. The wind blew off his hat and carried it out to sea.
   ....
   ....
8. Somebody will have to pay for the damage.
   ....
   ....
9. Oil drillers have discovered oil off the coast of Turkey.
   ....
   ....
10. The builders should have finished the house three months ago.
    ....
    ....

1.4 How a book is born

Look at the pictures showing the process involved in the birth of a book and complete the passage describing this process using the verbs in the box below. The first gap has been filled for you.

lay out	read	print	design
buy	draw up	deliver	check
accept	sign	send	set

First of all, someone has an idea for a book and sends a sample chapter to a publisher. The sample chapter (1) *is read* and, if all goes well, (2) .... Next a contract (3) .... and, if it's acceptable to the author, (4) .... by both parties. A delivery date for the manuscript (5) .... in the contract and, after months or years of work, the manuscript (6) .... to the publisher. Then the book cover (7) .... and the pages and chapters (8) .... as they should appear in the final book. When everything (9) .... carefully to make sure there are no mistakes, the book (10) .... Eventually, the book (11) .... to bookshops, where the author hopes it (12) .... by a great many people!

STUDY TIP

PASSIVES

- At the end of a passive sentence, don't write '*by someone*' or put the agent if it's obvious,
  e.g. The window was broken ~~by someone~~.
  We were taught the passive ~~by the teacher~~.
- The passive is very commonly used to describe a process,
  e.g. making biscuits ('Sugar and colourings are now added'); delivering a letter ('the letter is then collected'), etc.

2 Causative HAVE and GET (Study box, page 202)

Problems, problems, ...

Look at the following problems and decide what each person should **have done** to solve them. The first one is shown as an example.

1 My hair keeps getting in my eyes.
   You should have it cut.
2 The engine of Sarah's car is making a strange hissing noise.
   ....
   ....
3 Willy has got a roll of film with his holiday photos on.
   ....
   ....
4 Some children have just broken Mrs Moon's kitchen window.
   ....
   ....
5 Edgar keeps getting headaches when he reads the newspaper.
   ....
   ....
6 Marilyn is going abroad soon and has just discovered her passport expired last week!
   ....
   ....
7 Max has just done a translation but he's not sure about a few phrases.
   ....
   ....
8 Rupert has got a terrible pain in his ankle; he thinks it may be broken.
   ....
   ....
9 Edith thinks she might be going slightly deaf.
   ....
   ....
10 Water is pouring out of Sonia's washing machine.
   ....
   ....

STUDY TIP

CAUSATIVE 'HAVE'

- This form can also have a different meaning connected with unpleasant events/actions, e.g. Brian <u>had his nose broken</u> in a fight. Mary <u>had her handbag stolen</u> on the train.
- <u>get</u> is also possible instead of <u>have</u>, particularly in informal spoken English, e.g. I must <u>get</u> my car serviced.

3 Prepositional phrases (Study box, page 203)

Match and add

Match the first and second half of each of the ten sentences below and put an appropriate prepositional phrase in the spaces provided. Look at the example in number one.

according to	except for	as regards
in addition to		instead of
on account of	as far as	in spite of
apart from		by means of

1 In addition to being a pilot and rally driver,   D
2 .... transport,
3 .... local legend,
4 The only way of getting to the monastery
5 I've eaten nothing all day
6 .... I know,
7 .... asking for directions,
8 Sam was suspended from school
9 We didn't do much last weekend
10 Amanda carried on skiing

UNIT 11

A there's a witch in the woods.
B .... a pear for lunch.
C .... his constant bullying of younger boys.
D Sally is now learning to sail as well.
E .... hurting her knee in a fall.
F .... mowing the lawn.
G we'll have to go by bus.
H was .... an ancient chair-lift.
I we carried on, hoping we'd come across the place by luck.
J shops should be open as usual tomorrow.

4 Gerund and infinitive (Focus on grammar, pages 206–7)

Right or wrong?

Decide if the gerund and infinitive are used correctly or not in the following sentences. If you think there is a mistake, correct it. The first one has been done for you.

1 I'll never forget ~~to meet~~ *meeting* Mick Jagger after a concert in Dublin in 1984.
2 A: My computer doesn't seem to work.
  B: Have you tried plugging it in?
3 I regret informing you that your application for the post of manager has not been successful.
4 Will you remember buying the cake for the party, or had I better do it?
5 I was just starting getting interested in the film when there was a power cut.
6 A lot of people stopped eating eggs during the salmonella scare.
7 That cut looks quite deep, I'd say it needs to look at.
8 Oh look, the apple blossom has just started coming out. How lovely!
9 I regret saying all those nasty things to her now.
10 Would you like coming with us on holiday to Morocco?
11 They weren't sure of the way so they stopped asking for directions.
12 I like going to the dentist's at least once a year if possible.
13 Now, you won't forget sending us a postcard, will you?
14 Can't you stop asking so many questions?
15 OK, just try relaxing. How can I hypnotise you if you're so tense?

5 Wordcheck

Shopping

Fill in the missing words in the grid to reveal a word closely connected with shopping. One is shown as an example.

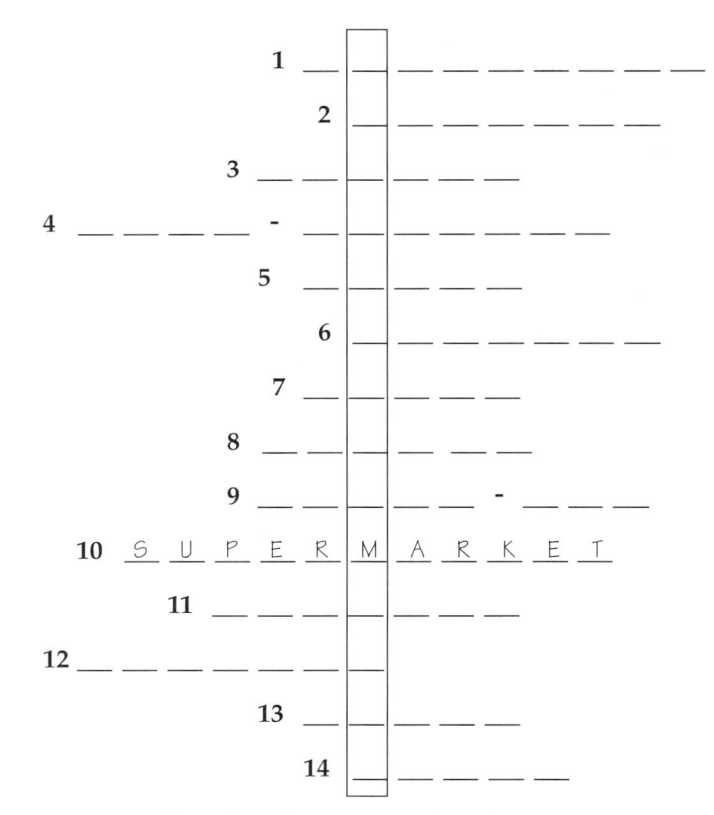

```
 1  _ _ _ _ _ _ _
 2    _ _ _ _ _ _
 3   _ _ _ _ _ _ _
 4 _ _ _ _ - _ _ _ _ _ _
 5    _ _ _ _ _
 6     _ _ _ _ _ _ _
 7    _ _ _ _ _
 8   _ _ _ _ _ _
 9    _ _ _ _ _ - _ _ _
10  S U P E R M A R K E T
11   _ _ _ _ _ _ _
12 _ _ _ _ _ _ _ _
13    _ _ _ _ _
14     _ _ _ _
```

1 A printed list of products you can buy from a company.
2 An exhibition of products in a shop to attract buyers.
3 By buying in bulk you may make a considerable ....
4 A shop where you help yourself.
5 If you see something you like in number 1, you place one.
6 A large metal container on wheels which you push around and fill with shopping.
7 The long narrow space where you walk between products in a shop.
8 A metal or plastic container with a handle which you put your shopping in in a shop.
9 Where you go to pay for your shopping when you leave.
10 A large store selling food, household products, etc.
11 The piece of paper you receive when you've paid for your shopping.
12 Something bought at a lower price than usual.
13 The store of goods a shop keeps available for sale.
14 Where the products are placed in most shops.

6 Grammar round-up

In the following questions complete the second sentence so it has a similar meaning to the first sentence. Use the word given and other words to complete each sentence. You must use between two and five words. Do not change the word given. The first one has been done for you.

1 The police have arrested the company treasurer for fraud.
  has
  The company treasurer *has been arrested* for fraud.

2 Although he saw the warning sign, he didn't slow down.
   spite
   He didn't slow down .... the warning sign.
3 Did I lock the door before I left? I'm not sure.
   remember
   I .... the door before I left.
4 Dorian is planning to get a famous artist to paint his portrait.
   painted
   Dorian is planning to .... by a famous artist.
5 Nobody will ever find the murder weapon in that deep water.
   never
   The murder weapon .... in that deep water.
6 Sally did quite well in her exams – she only failed geography.
   apart
   Sally did quite well in her exams .... geography.
7 Bob is sorry he argued with his best friend about such a small thing.
   regrets
   Bob .... with his friend about such a small thing.
8 Someone should change the light bulb in the bathroom before the guests arrive.
   needs
   The light bulb in the bathroom .... before the guests arrive.
9 People think Maurice owns a large villa in the south of France.
   thought
   Maurice .... a large villa in the south of France.
10 Why don't you ask Murray – he probably knows where you left it.
   try
   You .... Murray – he probably knows where you left it.

UNIT 12

1 Wishes and regrets (Focus on grammar, pages 210–211)

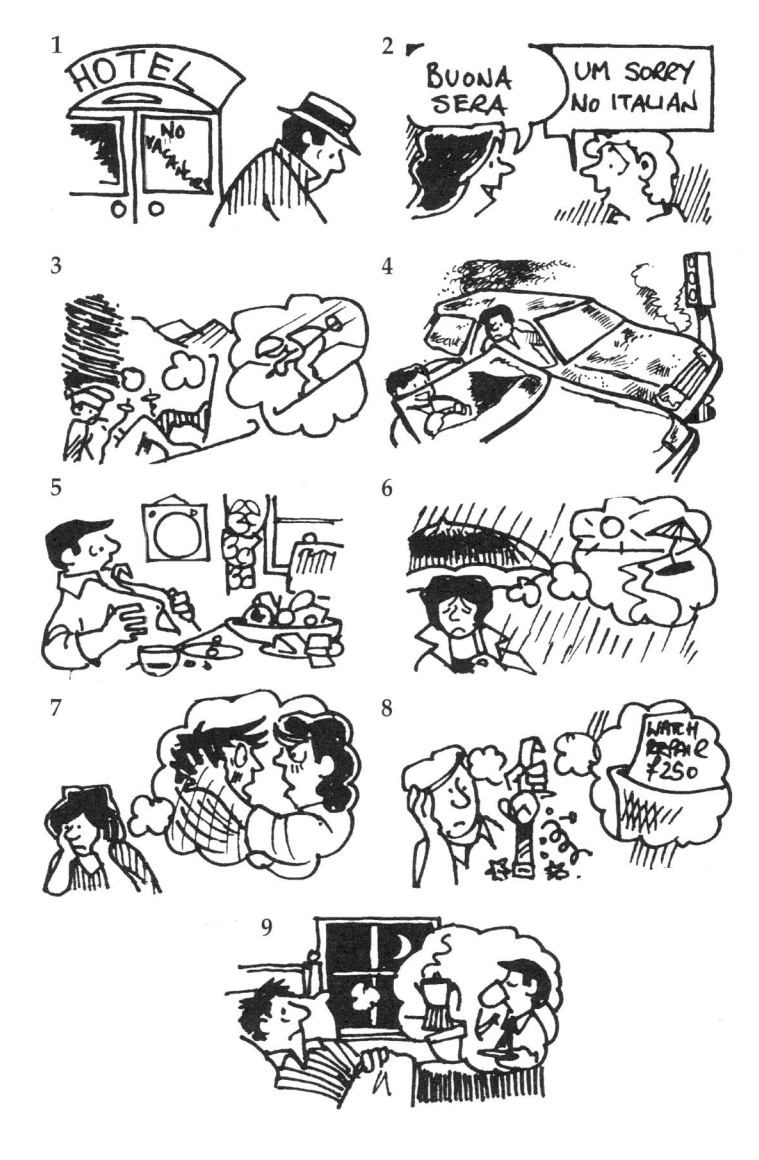

I wish, I wish, I wish …

What do you imagine the people in the following pictures are thinking? Write sentences to express their wishes and regrets. The first one is shown as an example.

1 I wish I'd booked a room!
2 If only ....
3 ....
4 ....
5 ....
6 ....
7 ....
8 ....
9 ....

UNIT 12

2 Past tense but present idea (Focus on grammar, pages 210–211)

What do you say?

What words would you use to express the following thoughts? Complete the sentences, as in number one.

1. It's half past midnight and you and your friend have to get up at 7a.m.
   Hey, come on. It's time *we went to bed.*

2. You're trying to convince your friend that it would be a good idea to have a burglar alarm installed.
   But suppose ....
   ....

3. You think you may have telephoned someone at an inconvenient time.
   Would you rather ....
   ....?

4. A shop assistant seems to think you don't understand and is speaking to you extremely slowly.
   There's no need to treat me as ....
   ....

5. Your brother said he'd repair the back door three months ago.
   It's high time ....
   ....

6. Your next door neighbour keeps parking his van in front of your gate.
   I'd rather ....
   ....

STUDY TIP

WISH

- <u>Wish</u> can only refer to the present or the past.
- To refer to the future, use <u>hope</u>.
- Keep a note of those verbs and phrases that take the past to refer to the present, e.g. wish, it's time, etc.

---

3 Conditional 3 (Focus on grammar, pages 217–218)

3.1 What if …?

Using the information in the following sentences, write sentences to say what could have happened if things had been different. The first one has been done for you.

1. Polly gave up smoking and got rid of that terrible cough she had.
   If *she hadn't given up smoking she wouldn't have got rid of that terrible cough she had.*

2. We missed the start of the show because we went to the wrong theatre first.
   We wouldn't ....
   ....

3. Tina was wearing her seat-belt and so she wasn't badly injured in the crash.
   If ....
   ....

4. The *Titanic* only sank because it hit an iceberg.
   If ....
   ....

5. The car broke down so we couldn't go away at the weekend.
   We'd ....
   ....

6. Rudy got badly sunburnt because he didn't put on any suntan lotion.
   He wouldn't ....
   ....

7. Because they called the fire brigade promptly most of the building was saved.
   The building ....
   ....

8. Dale happened to look up and saw the gunman on the roof.
   If he ....
   ....

3.2 Now or then?

Expand the following sentences into type 3 or mixed conditionals. Look at the example in the first one.

1. If Carla/not see/the car, she/may be/run over.
   If Carla hadn't seen the car, she might have been run over.

2. If we/take/the express train, we/be/there now!
   ....
   ....

3. I/fall/into the ravine/if Angus/not grab/my hand.
   ....
   ....

4. Amy still/be working/at the supermarket check-out if she/not decide/to emigrate to Canada last year.
   ....
   ....

5. We/be/in hospital with the others if we/eat/that strange meat last night.
   ....
   ....

6   If you/not forget/the map, we/not be/lost now!
    ....
    ....

7   I/visit/Isadora when I went to Madrid if I/not leave/my address book at home.
    ....
    ....

8   If I/not be/put in an incubator immediately after birth, I/not be/here today!
    ....
    ....

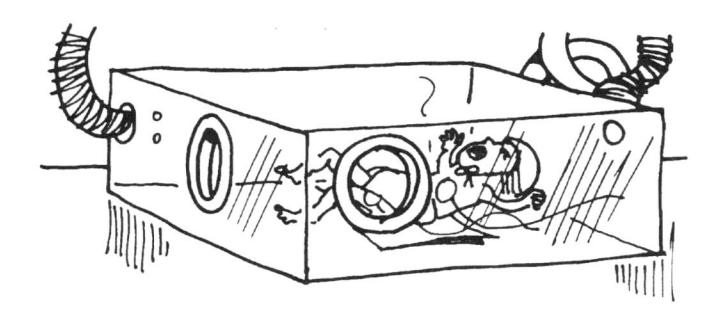

> **STUDY TIP**
>
> TYPE 3 CONDITIONAL
> - Remember that this refers to the opposite of what really happened, that's why it's often called the impossible condition,
>   e.g. If she'd seen the dog ...,
>   means she didn't see it.

4 Phrasal verbs with GIVE and TAKE (Study box, pages 216 and 220)

4.1 Match and add

Match the first half of the sentence in column A with the second half in column B, and add the correct form of a phrasal verb with either **give** or **take**. Look at the example provided in number one.

A

1   Ida *gave up* playing squash   [D]
2   It wasn't until 10 minutes after the plane had ....   [ ]
3   Simon's been putting on a lot of weight recently   [ ]
4   The teacher made Roger ....   [ ]
5   Journalists are very careful   [ ]
6   The instructor said she .... windsurfing [ ]
7   After five hours of lectures   [ ]
8   Quick! Get down to the record store –   [ ]
9   Erica seems rather distracted in class   [ ]

B

A   not to .... their sources of information.
B   they're .... free tickets for the open-air concert tomorrow.
C   and never .... her homework on time.
D   after she damaged her wrist.
E   so he's .... swimming to get back in shape.
F   all the things he'd stolen from the other children.
G   like a duck to water.
H   that he realised he'd left his briefcase in the airport toilet!
I   I was finding it hard to .... anything ....

4.2 Mistakes galore

In the following sentences the phrasal verbs have been mixed up. Sort out which verb should go where. See the example in number one.

1   The detective took ~~on~~ *off* his gloves to examine the piece of glass.
2   They had to give in their plan to climb the Matterhorn after Steve broke his leg.
3   Maggie took over a part-time job as a waitress to help pay the rent.
4   I find it very easy to take in to temptation when it comes to chocolates!
5   He was so charming that he managed to give them all up with his promises of big profits and no risk.
6   I see that multinational company took off another two small competitors last week.

5 Review of tenses (Focus on grammar, pages 221–222)

Put the verbs in brackets into a suitable (active or passive) tense and put any other words in the brackets in the right place. The first one has been done for you.

1. Our ferry *leaves* (leave) Santander at noon tomorrow.
2. I .... (get) fed up with Sam. He .... (always use) my razor.
3. I .... (not recognise) you if you .... (not say) hello. How much weight .... (you lose)?
4. Oh good! You .... (bring) your racket so we .... (be able) to have a game of squash over the weekend.
5. It was only after we .... (drive) for 10 minutes that we .... (remember) we .... (not lock) the front door.
6. We .... (have) a party next Friday. .... (do) you anything?
7. Janice .... (grow up) in the States, that's why she .... (spell) some words differently.
8. He .... (only just leave) school when he .... (make) his first million at the age of 19!
9. It's such a dangerous road there .... (be) a serious accident one of these days unless they .... (introduce) a speed limit.
10. I .... (come) next weekend if I .... (be) you. My parents .... (go) back to York by then.
11. They .... (work) on that book about Bath for ages. They .... (already/take) over 500 photographs!
12. Look, if I .... (know) where the place .... (be), I .... (tell) you. But I don't, so stop asking me!
13. She .... (share) her house with her brother at the moment. Apparently, he .... (just/evict) from his flat.
14. If he .... (not catch) stealing money red-handed, Clive .... (still/be) manager of the local bank.
15. Just think, this time last week we .... (ride) a camel in the desert.
16. It's my parents' wedding anniversary today. They .... (be) married for 40 years!
17. Brenda .... (take on) a full-time job last year when her husband .... (make) redundant from the company where he .... (work) for over 25 years.
18. I don't know what they .... (do) but they .... (hammer) away in the house next door since 8 o'clock this morning.

6 Wordcheck

Wedding Bells

Complete the crossword below. Two across has been done for you.

Across
2. What you give the happy couple. (7)
6. A woman is this on her wedding day. (5)
8. The group of people in the church for the wedding. (12)
10. Annual celebration of your wedding day. (11)
11. If you have promised to marry someone, you are .... (7)
12. The legally accepted relationship between a husband and wife. (8)
13. A formal act performed on an important social or religious occasion. (8)
14. Everybody eats a piece of this after the wedding. (4)

Down
1. A holiday taken by a man and woman who have just got married. (9)
3. Worn on the finger to show that you'll be faithful. (4)
4. A request that someone makes to a person they want to marry. (8)
5. An official piece of paper allowing you to do something. (7)
7. The formal ending of 12 across by law. (7)
8. A small church, or part of a church. (6)
9. What a man is called on his wedding day. (5)

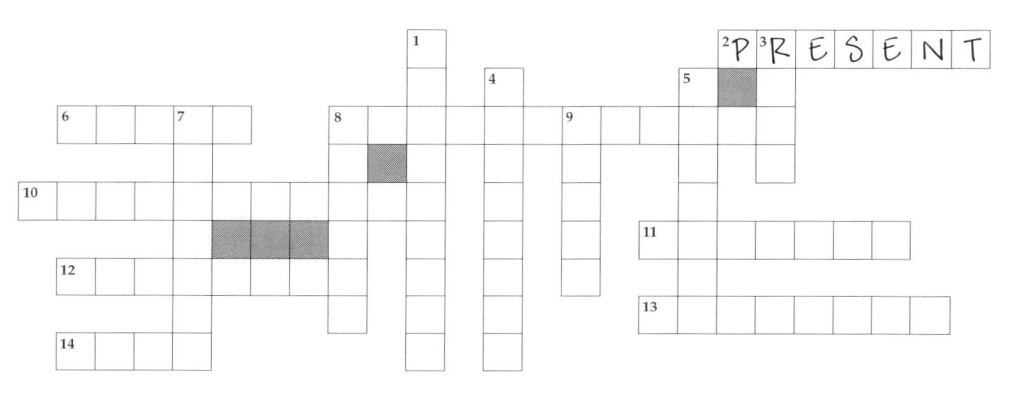

7 Grammar round-up

In the following questions complete the second sentence so it has a similar meaning to the first sentence. Use the word given and other words to complete each sentence. You must use between two and five words. Do not change the word given. The first one has been done for you.

1 We would prefer you not to smoke in the bedroom.
   rather
   We *would rather you did not/didn't* smoke in the bedroom.

2 I really regret not going to China when I had the chance to.
   wish
   I .... to China when I had the chance to.

3 I didn't cook anything because I didn't know you were coming.
   told
   If .... you were coming, I'd have cooked something.

4 She really resembles her mother, doesn't she?
   takes
   She really .... her mother, doesn't she?

5 You probably avoided having another quarrel by not seeing Kenny.
   had
   You .... another quarrel if you'd seen Kenny.

6 That wardrobe would be too big for our bedroom.
   take
   That wardrobe would .... too much space in our bedroom.

7 She only left her old job because she wasn't earning enough money.
   more
   She wouldn't have left her old job if she .... money.

8 My computer's ancient – how I'd like a new one!
   only
   My computer's ancient – .... a new one.

9 Nobody wanted our old fridge – not even for free.
   give
   We couldn't .... our old fridge.

10 Don't you think you'd better start revising for your exams?
   time
   Isn't .... revising for your exams?

Progress Test Four

UNITS 10–12

Check your progress by entering your score in the box at the end of each exercise and at the end of the complete test.

1 Read the text below and think of the word which best fits each space. Use only **one** word in each space.

The Mystery of the Melting Statue
The local police were completely mystified by the case. Lord Harrington's priceless crystal statue had disappeared in (1) .... of a sophisticated alarm system, which (2) .... have been activated if the statue had been lifted off its pedestal. In fact, the alarm had (3) .... off but only several minutes after the statue had been stolen and, (4) .... the time he got to the room, the security guard found all the windows and doors securely locked but … no statue! There were no clues in the room, (5) .... from some water on and around the pedestal where the statue had been. So, how had the crime been (6) .... out? After six weeks of going (7) .... the statements taken from everyone who lived and worked at Harrington Hall, the local police (8) .... up. They could think of no way of explaining the disappearance, (9) .... for one humorous young officer who suggested the statue (10) .... have melted as it was such a warm day for January! It was then that the case was (11) .... over by Inspector Nick Cavillon of Scotland Yard. Within three days the case had been solved and the thief (12) .... !
Interviewed shortly after the recovery of the statue, Inspector Cavillon explained how the crime had been committed. 'I remembered (13) .... of a similar case from some years ago. I mightn't have remembered it if a young detective had (14) .... made a joke about the statue melting. An extremely clever thief, Dexter Ross, known as the Iceman, had become famous for stealing crystal or cut-glass statues from museums all over the country. He was eventually caught and sent to prison for eight years. The way he stole the statues was by replacing them with statues made of ice of the same weight so (15) .... not to set off the alarm and (16) .... the guards wouldn't notice anything was wrong. In (17) .... to do this, he had to be extremely cool, calm and collected and have a very steady hand. He only ever worked in the

PROGRESS TEST FOUR

winter and at night, (18) .... he would have plenty of time to get away (19) .... the statue melted and set the alarm off. At Harrington Hall he probably only just got out in time as he hadn't reckoned on such warm weather.
(20) .... we knew who the criminal was, it was quite simple to find him as he'd gone back to his old job in an ice-cream factory!'

[20]

2 Read the following text. Look carefully at each line. Some of the lines are correct and some have a word which should not be there. If a line is correct, put a tick (✓) on the dotted line as in the examples. If a line has a word which should not be there, write the word on the dotted line, as in the examples.

A problem of communication

I can well remember trying to learn a foreign language ....✓....
at school. It must have had been the 'teach them, test   had
them, beat them' method. My teacher never explained   1 ....
why we were being taught this language or so that it   2 ....
might be important in the real life and not just for   3 ....
exams! If only I'd have known, I'd have tried a lot   4 ....
harder. I only found out years later during when I was   5 ....
driving in rural France and I needed to have got my   6 ....
car repaired. In the cities I always found someone   7 ....
who had understood some English but in that little   8 ....
village nobody did, least of all the garage mechanic!   9 ....
All I could do was use sign language until at the last   10 ....
he realised what the problem was.

[10]

3 Fill each blank with a suitable form of the word in brackets. See the example provided.

Example: Neil isn't very *interested* (interest) in his job.

1 There was a loud .... (explode) when they detonated the bomb.
2 Their .... (friend) started when they were at university together.
3 The company will pay for your lunch if you've still got the .... (receive).
4 There's a slight .... (possible) of rain tomorrow morning.
5 Mr Bean led a very normal .... (excite) life before he won £1,000,000 on the pools.
6 There are miles and miles of beautiful .... (spoil) sandy beaches along the south coast.
7 You need special .... (qualify) to become an engineer.
8 They said my clothing was .... (suit) and refused to let me into the club.
9 Miraculously, Judy walked away from the car crash completely .... (hurt)!
10 Ned thought parachuting was the most .... (fright) experience of his life and says he'll never try it again!

[10]

4 Choose the word or phrase which best completes each of the following sentences. Put a circle round the letter you choose as in the example.

Example: I .... I'll pass the exam.
A wish **B** want **C** like **(D)** hope

1 If that tooth is still giving you trouble, you'd better go to the dentist, ... you?
A wouldn't **B** didn't **C** hadn't **D** don't

2 Josh has taken .... swimming as he's got a bad back.
A up **B** on **C** in **D** off

3 Amy had no relatives except .... a distant cousin in Singapore.
A of **B** from **C** to **D** for

4 She said she tore the photograph in two .... accident but I'm not so sure.
A for **B** by **C** in **D** from

5 We had no complaints at all last year, ... we?
A hadn't **B** did **C** didn't **D** had

6 .... they didn't want to talk to us, but they became very friendly later on.
A Before **B** Firstly **C** Previously **D** At first

7 I .... you didn't tell Mick about this next time you see him.
A wish **B** regret **C** 'd rather **D** hope

8 While on holiday in Tunisia, I went .... food-poisoning.
A down with **B** through **C** in for **D** with

9 It .... have seen Sue you saw. She's in Poland at the moment.
A shouldn't **B** mightn't **C** can't **D** mustn't

10 You can pick up some fantastic .... in the sales just now.
A occasions **B** savings **C** displays **D** bargains

[10]

TOTAL [50]

Answer Key

UNIT 1

1.1

2 freezes 3 am/'m freezing 4 go; am/'m going 5 are you always leaving; makes 6 does your plane take off 7 Do you speak; am/'m learning; is/'s teaching 8 is/'s working; comes or is/'s coming 9 arrive 10 Are you coming; starts 11 is/'s always asking; never pays 12 are you doing; am/'m making 13 is/'s standing; is she wearing 14 are/'re constantly arguing/constantly argue 15 is/'s knocking; am/'m having

1.2

2H 3F 4A 5B 6C 7D 8E

2.1

2 which/that sells electrical goods. 3 who/that discovered radium? 4 whose car you crashed into last week.
5 who/that painted the ceiling of the Sistine Chapel.
6 who/that pay her compliments. 7 whose designer used to work with my brother. 8 who/that broke the window.
9 which/that causes malaria. 10 whose wife used to be a professional wrestler?

2.2

2 Liza Minnelli, whose mother was Judy Garland, became famous for her part in the film *Cabaret*.
3 The old van (that/which) Andy bought 10 years ago has never broken down.
4 None of the people (that/who) Hideyuki and Kanako met in Australia spoke a word of Japanese.
5 Pelé, whose real name is Edson Arantes do Nascimento, was the greatest footballer in the world.
6 Elvis Presley, who died in 1977, was known as the King of rock 'n' roll.
7 Not all of the people who/that take this exam pass it!
8 The strange orange-coloured soup (that/which) they gave us had been made by their grandmother.
9 Mickey Mouse, whose original name was Mortimer, first appeared in a cartoon in 1928.
10 Japanese, which uses three different types of script, is rather difficult for foreigners to learn to write.

2.3

2 Wrong – My hair, which started going grey when I was 25, is … . 3 Wrong – My TV, which I bought second-hand, has … .
4 Right 5 Right – (Alternatively: Peter! Here's someone that/who I … .) 6 Right 7 Right – as long as I have only one brother! – (No alternative) 8 Wrong – The Vatican, which is in Rome, is … . 9 Right 10 Wrong – Did you know that people that/who come from Manchester are …?

2.4

2 Greta found her engagement ring, which had belonged to her husband's great grandmother, under the sofa.
3 The Taj Mahal, which was built as a monument to a man's dead wife, is one of India's most famous sights.
4 No change.
5 The exhibition, which takes place every year, is always very successful.
6 Ambra phoned me to tell me that the cake I had made for her party had made everybody feel sick. (relative pronoun omitted)
7 We went to the Sydney Opera House, which is the city's most famous landmark.
8 No change.
9 No change *or* That's the man we saw …. (relative pronoun omitted)
10 Alcatraz, where America's most dangerous criminals used to be kept, is now a major tourist attraction.

3

2 live on 3 caught on 4 live up to 5 caught on 6 live on
7 caught up with 8 lived through 9 catch up with
10 caught on

4

2 D about 3 E with 4 A with 5 B in 6 G with
7 C with 8 F at/by

5.1

2H 3I 4C 5A 6J 7D 8E 9G 10B

5.2

2 fishing rod or net 3 jug 4 telescope 5 notepad or notebook 6 whistle 7 first-aid kit 8 scissors 9 scarf
10 iron

6

2 do you do 3 am/'m working temporarily 4 caught on
5 his sister for breaking/having broken 6 Venice, which is
7 live up to 8 is playing 9 were (very) excited about
10 are/'re always complaining about

UNIT 2

1.1

2 hard 3 terribly 4 happily 5 definitely 6 loud 7 strange, good 8 bad 9 careful 10 unfortunate

1.2

2,4,5,7 = adjectives   3,6,8 = adverbs

1.3

2 more intelligent 3 the cheapest 4 the most attractively 5 less tiring 6 more quietly 7 the happiest 8 harder 9 worse 10 more thinly

2.1

2 when–D, 3 ago–G, 4 before–H, 5 in–A, 6 for–B, 7 on–C, 8 on–E

2.2

2 moved/came 3 in 4 joined 5 while 6 obtain/get 7 until 8 included 9 was/had 10 received/won 11 played/performed/sang 12 By 13 appeared 14 received/won 15 died

2.3

A bred, fed, led, read, said, spread 2 fed 3 led
B laid, made, mislaid, paid 1 laid 2 mislaid
C brought, bought, caught, fought, thought 1 caught 2 fought
D bent, went, lent, meant, sent, spent 1 meant 2 bent 3 lent
E blew, drew, flew, grew, threw 1 drew 2 blew 3 grew
F bore, saw, swore, tore, wore 1 swore 2 tore 3 bore
G crept, kept, leapt, slept, swept, wept 1 wept 2 crept 3 swept

3.1

circle A = make   circle B = do

3.2

2 do; harm 3 do me a favour 4 make phone calls 5 do the washing-up 6 made fun of 7 made an excuse 8 did a course 9 make the bed 10 making trouble 11 make a wish

4.1

2 was repairing my car 3 was having lunch/eating a pizza 4 was having a drink 5 was sleeping 6 was having/taking a shower

4.2

2 were you doing … was assassinated 3 got lost … were walking 4 was walking … attacked 5 found … was digging 6 were having … got 7 were eating … were stealing 8 arrived … rushed 9 were gathering … was blowing 10 was leaving/left … went off

5

3,4,7,9 = the

6

2 put … on 3 put … through 4 put aside 5 put on 6 put up with 7 put … off 8 put … up 9 put … away 10 put out

7

2 salary 3 uniform 4 career 5 vacancy 6 apprentice 7 allowance 8 strike 9 wage packet 10 health hazard

8

2 put him up 3 swims better than 4 made the most 5 making enquiries into 6 while (I was) going/walking/while on my way 7 sang (really) beautifully 8 slowly and (I) wrote illegibly 9 put off 10 make sure

UNIT 3

1.1

2 has been 3 has had 4 have lost/broken 5 have lost/forgotten 6 has been 7 hasn't smoked 8 have spent

1.2

2 H have arrived so far 3 A have you lived here for? 4 E have just arrived from Spain? 5 C have they already repaired? 6 B has he typed up to now? 7 F have we been here before? 8 G has she had since Monday?

1.3

(suggested answers only) 2 Have you ever tried 'sushi'? 3 When did you see Susan? 4 How long have you worked here (for)? 5 Did you enjoy your holiday in Egypt? 6 How many times have you been to Australia? 7 What did you think of the film? 8 Have you ever been to Romania?

2

2 depends on 3 rely on 4 disapproved of 5 complaining about 6 reminds … about 7 listen to; warned … about 8 opposite to 9 paying for 10 concentrating on

3.1

2 has been raining 3 has been smoking 4 has been trying 5 have been sunbathing 6 Have … been fighting 7 has been peeling 8 have been practising

3.2

2 have been 3 have … been going out with 4 has … lived 5 haven't worked 6 has … been talking 7 have … eaten 8 has been snowing 9 have been working/have worked 10 has played 11 has been driving, hasn't had 12 hasn't seen 13 has rented/has been renting 14 have been going over 15 Have … lived

4

(suggested answers only) 2 round black plastic 3 cylindrical metal 4 small round china 5 large white cotton 6 long thin wooden

5

2 was able to 3 can/'ll be able to 4 was able to 5 be able to 6 couldn't 7 has been able to 8 could 9 couldn't 10 be able to 11 were able to 12 could have 13 could 14 couldn't 15 can

6

2 80-year-old 3 three-year 4 30-hour 5 three-week 6 four-minute 7 five-bedroom 8 four-litre

7.1

2 exhilarating 3 aggressive 4 absorbed 5 competitive 6 claustrophobia 7 disappointment 8 elation 9 tension 10 peace of mind

7.2

2 climbing 3 golf 4 tennis 5 judo 6 skating 7 swimming 8 windsurfing 9 shot put 10 rugby 11 baseball 12 body building

go – running, climbing, skating, swimming, windsurfing
play – golf, tennis, rugby, baseball
do – judo, shot put, body building

8

2 has worked/been working here (for) 3 a big red French 4 reminded me (greatly) of 5 although/but she could have been 6 has already been 7 because she has/'s been playing 8 were able to clean up 9 a 50-dollar fine 10 has been working there since

ANSWERS TO PROGRESS TEST ONE

1

(Score 1 point for each correct answer.) **1** won **2** year
3 which **4** who **5** to **6** hard **7** each/every
8 mile/kilometre **9** lunch **10** on **11** with **12** managed
13 delighted **14** did/has given **15** reminded
16 doing/practising **17** off **18** racket **19** put **20** can

2

(Score 1 point for each correct answer.) **1** of **2** are **3** ✓
4 it **5** ✓ **6** the **7** ✓ **8** been **9** not **10** ✓

3

1 D **2** A **3** B **4** A **5** D **6** C **7** D **8** B **9** A **10** C

4

(Score 1 point for each correct answer.) **1** friendly
2 Unfortunately **3** taught **4** truly **5** disapprove **6** flown
7 farthest/furthest **8** broken **9** better **10** tore

UNIT 4

1
2 robbed 3 robbed ... of 4 stole ... from 5 robbing
6 stealing 7 stolen from 8 rob ... of

2
2 don't have/need to 3 should/ought to 4 needn't
5 have to 6 should have 7 had to 8 needn't have
9 shouldn't have 10 mustn't 11 didn't need to/didn't have
to 12 needn't have 13 must 14 mustn't 15 have to

3.1
2 got (a)round 3 broke into; broke up 4 got away with
5 get away 6 broke off 7 got ... back 8 get at 9 getting at
10 broke down

3.2
2 broke through – A 3 F – get by 4 B – got away with
5 broke down – G 6 broken up – H 7 E – get ... across
8 C – break out

4.1
2 broken 3 acquired 4 fascinating 5 exciting 6 written
7 winning 8 embarrassing 9 smiling 10 baked

4.2
(in any order) 2 Walking down the High Street, she met an old school friend. 3 The person given the job was the boss's nephew! 4 Looking for a short cut, I got completely lost in the woods. 5 Looking through the keyhole, I could see the body lying on the floor. 6 Having read the book, he decided not to see the film. 7 The painting stolen from the art gallery was only a copy worth very little. 8 Having won the race, she was disqualified for pushing.

5
2 short-sighted 3 left-handed 4 tight-fitting 5 long-sighted
6 badly-dressed 7 short-sleeved 8 badly-behaved

6
Across
4 lookout 6 confess 9 arrest 10 suspended 12 hold-up
14 accuse 16 gun
Down
2 report 3 loitering 5 witness 7 sentence 8 vandal
11 burglar 12 hostage 13 haul 15 court

7
2 do not/don't have to 3 got away with 4 having seen the 5 knowing how to say it 6 needn't/need not have worn
7 broke down 8 have to wear 9 get me down
10 well-dressed

UNIT 5

1.1

2 get … touch **3** drop … lands **4** don't put … stops **5** floats … pour **6** hold … dies **7** die … don't give **8** drop … breaks

1.2

2 Drive carefully if it's foggy. **3** Take an aspirin if you've got a headache. **4** If it's your first day at the beach, don't sunbathe for too long. **5** Give me a ring if you need a hand. **6** If the baby cries, don't pick him up. **7** Call the doctor if the pain gets worse. **8** If you've seen the film, tell us what it's about. **9** Go to bed if you've done the washing-up. **10** Move closer to the blackboard if you can't see.

1.3

2 Unless **3** Suppose **4** unless **5** as long as/provided **6** Suppose **7** Unless **8** as long as/provided

2

2 by herself **3** out of reach **4** by boat/ship **5** out of doors **6** out of control **7** in sight **8** out of sight **9** in reach/sight **10** under control

3

2 The scissors are broken. **3** The crossroads are blocked. **4** His clothes have shrunk. **5** Kevin's shorts are ripped. **6** This maths is difficult. **7** The news is depressing. **8** The contents of the fridge have gone bad. **9** The centre is old but the outskirts are modern. **10** Michael's clothes are too big.

4

(suggested answers only) 2 Well, if he wore glasses, he wouldn't get headaches. **3** Well, if she took some exercise, she wouldn't get fat. **4** Well, if you studied more, you wouldn't fail. **5** Well, if you stayed in on Sunday night, you wouldn't find it so difficult to get up on Monday morning. **6** Well, if she gave up smoking, she wouldn't have a cough. **7** Well, if they got an emergency passport, they'd be able to travel abroad. **8** Well, if he worked less, he'd probably live longer!

5

2 set up **3** wore off **4** set down **5** sets in **6** set off **7** wear out **8** set off

6.1

2 Strange – Can I have a glass of water, Mum? **3** OK **4** Strange – I wonder if I might borrow £250,000, Mr Scott? **5** Strange – Can I borrow your pen for a moment, Pete? **6** OK

6.2

2 I wonder if I could open the window? **3** May I have a look at that vase? **4** Can I get a coke? **5** Could I use your phone? **6** Can I have an apple?

7.1

2 D **3** I **4** B/J **5** K **6** C **7** A **8** L **9** F **10** G **11** H **12** B/J

7.2

2 dispose **3** layers **4** junk mail **5** packaging **6** Convenience **7** disposable **8** throw-away

8

2 wonder if I could **3** provided that you do not/don't **4** set up the company **5** were you, I would/'d buy **6** earnings this year have been/are **7** you can camp **8** set off **9** was Vicki's favourite subject **10** if it is/'s sunny

UNIT 6

1

2 does … start 3 is going to be 4 're going to crash
5 's going to be 6 takes off 7 are … playing 8 are … doing
9 are arriving 10 'm meeting 11 's going to have 12 'm going to jump

2

(*means only the contracted form ('ll) is possible) 2 'll
3 Shall 4 'll/will; won't 5 shall 6 *'ll 7 won't 8 *'ll

3.1

(suggested answers only) 2 I hope I'll have a good job. 3 I think I'll speak good English. 4 I'm sure I'll have a nice house. 5 I don't think I'll be a millionaire. 6 I expect I'll be married. 7 Maybe I'll have some children. 8 I'm sure I won't be living abroad. 9 I imagine there will be more space travel. 10 I hope there will be no tooth decay. 11 I don't think there will be another world war. 12 There could be genetically-engineered babies.

3.2

2 'll be having 3 'll be flying 4 'll have been flying 5 'll have seen 6 'll have been touring 7 'll be seeing 8 'll be taking off 9 'll have tasted 10 'll have been 11 'll be enjoying 12 'll be 13 'll have visited 14 'll have taken; 'll have bought

4

2 The doctor warned her she had to cut down on her smoking. 3 Although they cut across town, it took them longer than going round the ring-road. 4 She promised to help us but, as usual, she let us down at the last moment.
5 The company was prevented from cutting down the trees to make way for a new supermarket car park. 6 As it was her first offence, the magistrate let her off with a suspended sentence. 7 One of my jobs on the farm was to let out the chickens every morning at 7a.m. 8 The chef cut up the meat into small cubes before putting it in the pan. 9 The accident was caused by the taxi driver, who cut in in front of the bus and then braked suddenly. 10 You have seven days in which to pay your bill, after which time your gas supply will be cut off. 11 Rapunzel let down her long hair so that her lover could climb up the tower to her window!

5

1 television 2 disk 3 keypad 4 patent 5 robot
6 computer 7 printer 8 dial 9 pager 10 plug in
11 switch off 12 keyboard 13 monitor 14 screen
The hidden word is VIDEOTELEPHONE.

6

2 is going to sell 3 will/'ll never do it 4 are you doing
5 cut down on 6 will/'ll have finished 7 cut off 8 will have already 9 takes off 10 let down

ANSWER KEY

ANSWERS TO PROGRESS TEST TWO

1

(Score 1 point for each correct answer.) **1** Driving **2** was
3 had **4** going **5** have **6** broken **7** beginning/starting
8 were **9** on **10** shall/can/will **11** starts **12** 'll **13** steals
14 caring/worrying/thinking **15** set **16** control **17** aged
18 at **19** looking **20** let/gave

2

(Score 1 point for each correct answer.) **1** to **2** ✓ **3** will
4 to **5** an **6** ✓ **7** must/have to **8** ✓ **9** had **10** ✓

3

(Score 1 point for each correct answer.) **1** congestion
2 fitting **3** surroundings **4** hold-up **5** provided/providing
6 returnable **7** printer **8** acquired **9** Watching **10** recycling

4

(Score 1 point for each correct answer.) **1** B **2** B **3** D **4** A
5 C **6** C **7** C **8** B **9** C **10** A

UNIT 7

1

2 no; no 3 the; no 4 the; the 5 no; no 6 the 7 no
8 no; the 9 no 10 no; no; the

2.1

2 Flying 3 Skiing 4 swimming 5 Sunbathing 6 Biting
7 writing 8 hunting

2.2

2 After going 3 before going 4 after being 5 without
paying 6 for sticking 7 On hearing 8 from eating

2.3

2 doing F telling 3 playing A playing 4 meeting G
5 going I telling 6 telephoning/calling/contacting B wasting
7 stealing/taking J hitting 8 being D shouting/chanting
9 having C cutting/mowing 10 studying H finding

3

2 bring about 3 bring in 4 bringing out 5 bring … round

4

2 had been working 3 arrived 4 had forgotten
5 had agreed 6 was 7 met 8 had been working 9 was
10 hadn't been

5

2 playing 3 throw 4 move 5 cut down (they saw the
complete action) 6 sitting 7 building 8 swimming
9 throw

6

2 sleeping bag 3 flag 4 compass 5 money belt 6 suitcase
7 injection 8 traveller's cheque 9 camera 10 tent
11 insurance 12 hitch-hiking 13 visa 14 souvenir

7

2 Nina's phoning/phone call 3 had already won
4 noticed/saw the cat hiding 5 Diana break
6 without asking for 7 had been driving for
8 objects to getting/having to get
9 his shouting/his way of shouting
10 bring someone round

UNIT 8

1.1

(suggested answers) **2** too fat to fit in the bed. **3** tall enough to join the police (force). **4** too cold to swim in. **5** too poor to buy a new hi-fi. **6** too spicy to eat. **7** is too dangerous to drive. **8** too dark to play football. **9** old enough to drive a car. **10** too deaf to hear what you're saying. **11** fit enough to play tennis.

1.2

(suggested answers) **2** To remember them **3** to get away from the pollution **4** To phone a foreign country **5** to save time **6** To speak a foreign language **7** to overcome stress **8** to improve their pronunciation

1.3

2 no **3** to; to **4** to; no **5** no **6** to **7** to **8** no **9** no **10** to **11** no **12** to **13** no

2

2 look them up in your dictionary **3** looks in **4** looking after young children **5** look through/at **6** looked up to **7** look out **8** looking/to look for gold

3.1

2 But they guaranteed there would be no increase in the cost of using public transport. **3** But they said they were making great progress in cutting down pollution. **4** But they said old-age pensions would go up by at least 10 per cent. **5** But they told us they were going to provide more hospital services in every city. **6** But they stated they had signed agreements with 20 international companies. **7** But they said they had already started employment training programmes for school leavers. **8** But they promised to clean/they would clean up all our rivers and beaches.

3.2

2 Duncan suggested that we should go/went to Scotland for our holidays. **3** Liza's friend promised not to tell anyone about her secret. **4** Clint warned us not to walk around after dark as it could be very dangerous. **5** Angela invited me (to go) round for coffee. **6** The mechanic explained that the car wouldn't start because I had flooded the engine with petrol. **7** One of her students complained that he was not really learning anything with that method of teaching. **8** The children's mother asked them to put their toys away before they went to bed. **9** The tour guide advised us/warned us not to drink the tap water. **10** The old gardener warned us that the castle was haunted.

3.3

2 My client can't have committed the murder as he was seen 10 miles away at the time. **3** Don't forget to hand in your key before you leave. **4** Don't speak unless you're spoken to. **5** Do you remember that the company still hasn't paid for the last consignment of goods? **6** You must eat a strong local sausage called 'chorizo'. **7** Please don't throw litter into our garden. **8** Don't worry, I'll investigate/look into the matter. **9** Keep your tickets in case an inspector gets on. **10** Why don't you start by talking about your earliest memories?

4

2 get round to repairing **3** getting on very well **4** got over **5** get through to **6** get on with **7** get out of

5

2 The more careful the student, the fewer mistakes he/she makes. **3** The more perfect the diamond, the more expensive it is to buy. **4** The riper the plums, the sweeter they are to eat. **5** The colder the weather, the greater the chance of snow. **6** The more coffee Richard drinks, the more nervous he becomes. **7** The more quickly someone eats, the greater the chance of his/her getting indigestion. **8** The closer the house is to the centre, the more rent you have to pay.

6

2 the **3** no **4** no **5** the **6** the **7** the **8** the **9** the **10** no **11** no **12** the

7

2 only child **3** pocket money **4** ex-husband **5** household chores **6** housework **7** mod cons **8** family budget **9** career **10** growing up

8

2 heavier the package (is), the **3** us that our flight might **4** looked up to **5** is not/isn't big enough **6** gets out of going **7** Do not/Don't forget to take **8** for Suzy to reach **9** made the demonstrators leave **10** in order to make

UNIT 9

1.1

2 Wrong – some information   3 Right
4 Wrong – a trip   5 Right   6 Right   7 Wrong – furniture
8 Wrong – any money/a single penny   9 Wrong – hair is
10 Wrong – time   11 Right   12 Wrong – was

1.2

(those not possible) 2 A   3 C   4 B   5 A   6 B   7 B   8 A
9 B   10 B

2

2 I   3 J   4 L   5 M   6 N   7 C   8 B   9 A   10 D   11 O   12 K
13 F   14 E   15 G

3.1

2 I'd last bought an article of clothing.   3 I usually bought my clothes   4 was the most I'd ever spent on one article.   5 I was next going to buy some clothes   6 I'd ever visited Lennon's Fashion House   7 I'd like a Lennon's credit card   8 she could show me round Lennon's for 5 minutes.

3.2

I wonder if you could possibly tell me …
I wonder if you could tell me …
Could you possibly tell me …
Do you happen to know …
Can you tell me …
Do you know …

B (suggested answers) Do you know if this is a no-smoking area?   **C** I wonder if you could tell me how much a ticket costs?   **D** I wonder if you could possibly tell me how old you are?   **E** Can you tell me why you've given me a parking fine?
F Do you know which way the centre is?
G Do you happen to know what time the bank opens?
H Could you possibly tell me where the toilets are?

4

2 both; neither   3 either   4 none   5 none   6 all
7 all; each; either   8 every

5

2 F & I   3 B & H   4 C & J   5 A & E

6.1

(words can be given in any order – word group names do not have to be the same)
bandage, plaster, compress = dressings
graze, scratch, burn = injuries
protein, fibre, carbohydrates = nutrients/diet
treat, relieve, apply = verbs to do with first aid
cold, fever, flu = common illnesses
bruise, scab, blistering = things that appear on the skin
aspirin, antiseptic, injection = types of treatment

6.2

2 E   3 B   4 F   5 G   6 H   7 A   8 D

7

2 hardly any petrol   3 if I had ever considered   4 came up against   5 each child was   6 discouraged Steve from studying
7 large number of   8 came across   9 was a lack of   10 were you last night/yesterday evening

ANSWER KEY

ANSWERS TO PROGRESS TEST THREE

1

(Score 1 point for each correct answer.) 1 the 2 to 3 seeing/photographing 4 sitting/lying 5 were 6 hardly 7 look 8 came 9 had 10 lying/sitting/sunbathing/walking 11 To 12 up 13 climbing/coming 14 bring 15 looking/staring 16 if/whether 17 apologised 18 happened 19 lack 20 tent

2

(Score 1 point for each correct answer.) 1 disagrees 2 dressing 3 household 4 unhealthy 5 upbringing 6 neighbourhood 7 Accommodation 8 equipment 9 discouraged 10 mouthfuls

3

(Score 1 point for each correct answer.) 1 ✓ 2 had 3 ✓ 4 ✓ 5 how 6 far 7 ✓ 8 to 9 of 10 ✓

4

(Score 1 point for each correct answer.) 1 B 2 A 3 D 4 C 5 A 6 B 7 C 8 C 9 D 10 C

UNIT 10

1

2 Before 3 during 4 First 5 as soon as 6 Then 7 while
8 When 9 Meanwhile 10 until 11 after 12 during
13 By the time 14 later

2

2 For cleaning 3 (In order)/(so as) to eliminate
4 So that ... park 5 (So as)/(In order) to get

3

2 went down with 3 go with 4 went through 5 go in for
6 didn't go off 7 went on 8 went over/through
9 go without 10 going on

4

2 can't have got/received 3 can't be 4 might know
5 may/might/could rain 6 could have stolen
7 Might/Could ... have left 8 can help 9 must have ... forgotten 10 Could/Might ... have caused
11 must have heard 12 may/might/could be

5

2 by accident 3 on fire 4 At first 5 in danger 6 at the same time 7 At times 8 at last 9 out of danger 10 in the end
11 in difficulty

6

2 Right 3 Wrong – didn't she 4 Right 5 Right
6 Wrong – will you 7 Wrong – hadn't you 8 Wrong – has he
9 Right 10 Right 11 Wrong – will/would you
12 Wrong – aren't I 13 Right 14 Wrong – can they
15 Wrong – hadn't we

7

(odd word out) 2 shaking 3 decompression 4 gasp
5 shatter 6 thud 7 jinxed 8 limping 9 alertness 10 tangle

8

2 as soon as 3 so as not to make 4 might have taken 5 has (got) no chance 6 during your stay/holiday
7 will have gone off 8 must have been started
9 better report this, hadn't 10 woke the baby by accident

UNIT 11

1.1

2 is made by bees. 3 was invented by Marconi. 4 was sung/recorded/composed by the Beatles. 5 was sunk by an iceberg. 6 is made from flour and eggs. 7 was directed/made by Hitchcock. 8 is made from hops and barley. 9 was defeated at Waterloo. 10 was discovered by Columbus. 11 was composed by Verdi. 12 is played in Spain. 13 is made by worms. 14 was destroyed by a volcanic eruption. 15 was invented by Sony.

1.2

2 are not allowed beyond this point. 3 is (probably) going to be arrested. 4 will be/are accepted only with a guarantee card. 5 was built in 1888. 6 is being/going to be opened by the princess on Saturday. 7 was lost here on Saturday 4th and a reward is (being) offered. 8 will probably be promoted. 9 has been made in the treatment of cancer.
10 must be accompanied in the lift.

1.3

2 A priceless antique vase has been stolen from the British Museum. 3 This letter should not have been opened. It's private. 4 The cover of the book was accidentally printed upside-down. 5 The play is going to be performed outdoors.
6 The lecture hall is being used next Friday. 7 His hat was blown off and carried out to sea. 8 The damage will have to be paid for. 9 Oil has been discovered off the coast of Turkey.
10 The house should have been finished three months ago.

1.4

2 is accepted 3 is drawn up 4 is signed 5 is set
6 is delivered 7 is designed 8 are laid out 9 has been checked 10 is printed 11 is sent 12 will be bought

2

(suggested answers) 2 She should have it checked/looked at/repaired. 3 He should have it developed. 4 She should have it repaired. 5 He should have his eyes tested. 6 She should have it renewed. 7 He should have them checked. 8 He should have it x-rayed. 9 She should have her ears/hearing tested. 10 She should have it repaired.

3

2 As regards G 3 According to A 4 H by means of
5 B apart from or except for 6 As far as J 7 Instead of I
8 C on account of 9 F except for or apart from
10 E in spite of

4

2 Right 3 to inform 4 to buy 5 to get 6 Right 7 looking at
8 Right 9 Right 10 to come 11 to ask 12 to go 13 to send
14 Right 15 to relax

5

1 catalogue 2 display 3 saving 4 self-service 5 order
6 trolley 7 aisle 8 basket 9 check-out 10 supermarket
11 receipt 12 bargain 13 stock 14 shelf.
The hidden word is ADVERTISEMENTS.

6

2 in spite of seeing 3 don't remember locking 4 have/get his portrait painted 5 will never be found 6 apart from failing 7 regrets arguing 8 needs changing/to be changed
9 is thought to own 10 could try asking

UNIT 12

1

(suggested answers) **2** If only I spoke/could speak (some) Italian. **3** If only I could ski. **4** I wish I had a new/better/bigger car. **5** If only I hadn't eaten so much for lunch. **6** I wish I was/were on holiday. **7** If only I hadn't hit him. **8** If only I hadn't thrown the receipt away. **9** I wish I hadn't had coffee at dinner time.

2

2 But suppose someone broke into the house. **3** Would you rather I called at another time? **4** There's no need to treat me as if/though I was/were an idiot. **5** It's high time you repaired the back door. **6** I'd rather you didn't park your van in front of my gate.

3.1

2 We wouldn't have missed the start of the show if we hadn't gone to the wrong theatre first. **3** If Tina hadn't been wearing her seat-belt she might/would have been badly injured in the crash. **4** If the *Titanic* hadn't hit an iceberg it wouldn't have sunk. **5** We'd have gone away for the weekend if the car hadn't broken down. **6** He wouldn't have got so badly sunburnt if he'd put on suntan lotion. **7** The building wouldn't have been saved if they hadn't called the fire brigade so promptly. **8** If he hadn't happened to look up he wouldn't have seen the gunman on the roof.

3.2

2 If we'd taken the express train, we'd be there now! **3** I'd have fallen into the ravine if Angus hadn't grabbed my hand. **4** Amy would still be working at the supermarket check-out if she hadn't decided to emigrate to Canada last year. **5** We'd be in hospital with the others if we'd eaten that strange meat last night. **6** If you hadn't forgotten the map, we wouldn't be lost now! **7** I'd have visited Isadora when I went to Madrid if I hadn't left my address book at home. **8** If I hadn't been put in an incubator immediately after birth, I wouldn't be here today!

4.1

2 taken off **H** **3 E** taken up **4** give back **F** **5 A** give away **6** took to **G** **7 I** take ... in **8 B** giving away **9 C** gives in

4.2

2 give up **3** took on **4** give in **5** take ... in **6** took over

5

2 'm getting; 's always using **3** wouldn't have recognised; hadn't said; have you lost **4** 've brought; 'll be able **5** had been driving; remembered; hadn't locked
6 're having; Are you doing **7** grew up; spells **8** had only just left; made **9** 's going to be/'ll be; introduce **10** 'd come; were/was; will have gone **11** 've been working; 've already taken **12** knew; was/is; 'd tell **13** 's sharing; 's just been evicted **14** hadn't been caught; would still be **15** were riding **16** 've been married **17** took on; was made; had worked/been working **18** 're doing; 've been hammering

6

Across: **6** bride **8** congregation **10** anniversary **11** engaged **12** marriage **13** ceremony **14** cake
Down: **1** honeymoon **3** ring **4** proposal **5** licence **7** divorce **8** chapel **9** groom

7

2 really wish I had/'d gone **3** you/they had/'d told me/I'd been told **4** takes after **5** would/'d probably have had **6** take up **7** had/'d been earning more **8** if only I had **9** even give away **10** it time you started

ANSWER KEY

ANSWERS TO PROGRESS TEST FOUR

1

(Score 1 point for each correct answer) **1** spite **2** should
3 gone **4** by **5** apart **6** carried **7** over/through **8** gave
9 except **10** must/might/could/may **11** taken **12** arrested
13 hearing **14** not **15** as **16** so that **17** order **18** so
19 before **20** Once/Immediately/When

2

(Score 1 point for each correct answer.) **1** ✓ **2** so **3** the
4 have **5** during **6** got **7** ✓ **8** had **9** ✓ **10** the

3

(Score 1 point for each correct answer.) **1** explosion
2 friendship **3** receipt **4** possibility **5** unexciting
6 unspoilt **7** qualifications **8** unsuitable **9** unhurt
10 frightening

4

(Score 1 point for each correct answer.) **1** C **2** A **3** D **4** B
5 B **6** D **7** C **8** A **9** C **10** D